Queen of the Turf

QUEEN OF THE TURF
The Dorothy Paget story
Quintin Gilbey

Arthur Barker Limited
London
A subsidiary of Weidenfeld (Publishers) Limited

Arthur Barker Limited
11 St John's Hill, London SW11

35734

ISBN 0 213 16435 3

Printed in Great Britain by
Redwood Burn Limited, Trowbridge & Esher

Contents

Illustrations

Acknowledgements

Acknowledgements are due to the following for kind permission to reproduce the illustrations in this book : The Radio Times Hulton Picture Library; the Press Association Ltd; W. W. Rouch and Co; Central Press Photos Ltd; and Mrs J. Mann.

Part I

The D. P. legend

1

An uncontrollable child

The Honourable Dorothy Wyndham Paget was a living legend. Enormously rich, impossibly difficult and invariably eccentric, she attracted headlines wherever she went and whatever she did throughout her astonishing career. Indeed, although her greatest loves were horse-racing and motor-racing her notoriety spread far beyond these fields so that, between the thirties and her death in 1960, it is true to describe her as one of the most genuinely famous women in the world. It was a fame unlike that of a film star or a member of a royal family: it depended on herself, on those qualities – attractive and unattractive – which kept her a household name for a generation.

D.P., as she was known, was born in 1905, the daughter of Almeric Paget, later Lord Queenborough, who was himself a remarkable man. Packed off to America on his twenty-first birthday with a £5 note and instructions to make his fortune, he did so in record time by marrying one of the richest of American heiresses. She was Pauline, daughter of William C. Whitney, sportsman, politician, businessman and owner of a colossal fortune worth many millions. She bore Almeric two daughters, of whom Dorothy was the second, and could well afford to indulge little Dorothy, her favourite, which she did on a grandiose scale.

Young D.P. spent her early years in considerable luxury under the fond regime of her doting mother. Not surprisingly, she grew into a spoiled, unlovable child, close to her mother, distant from her father. Neither Lady Queenborough, nor the bevy of servants who waited on her daughters hand and foot, ever corrected Miss Dorothy – whatever her demands, delinquencies or tantrums. It was therefore a difficult, if not impossible, task which fell to poor Lord Queenborough when, shortly after Dorothy's twelfth birthday, his wife died and he was left to do what he could to bring a semblance of order to the unruly character which his self-willed daughter was developing. For her own part Dorothy was heartbroken : she had lost her mother, and in reaction became even more sullen and abominably rude to the servants, and to her father, than she had been before. It made Lord Queenborough's task no easier.

One obvious solution was education, and Dorothy was sent to Heathfield School. Here she proved as unco-operative with the mistresses of that exclusive academy for young ladies as she had been with her father, and they regretfully informed him that they could no longer try to educate a girl who refused to be educated. Five more schools followed in quick succession, and Dorothy was expelled from all of them.

In her adult life Dorothy Paget was an anachronistic, almost feudal character, and one wondered how she had managed to stray into the twentieth century; but in childhood she was decades before her time. Sixty years ago children did as they were told, with stern parents and sterner nannies leaving them in no doubt that children should be seen and not heard. Yet the first children's strike was more than half a century away when D.P. gave a demonstration of civil disobedience which shocked her fellow-pupils as much as it did her teachers. Schoolmistresses hesitate to punish a great heiress, but blandishments, pleadings and scoldings were like water off a duck's back to the thirteen-year-old D.P., who acted as if she had not heard them, and retired to bed.

I had a similar experience with her some fifteen years later. Her great horse Golden Miller had just won a small race at Wincanton, and I approached her on behalf of my readers

4

to ask if Golden Miller would be given another race before he went to Cheltenham to contest the Gold Cup. She completely ignored my query. I had never spoken to her before and I thought she might be a little hard of hearing so I repeated my question a little louder. She looked at me blankly so I asked her a third time at the top of my voice. My voice must have echoed round the paddock, but there was still no response. Like her teachers, I gave it up as a bad job.

I do not know who it was who, following D.P.'s whirlwind tour of the six most fashionable English girls' schools, suggested to Lord Queenborough that a Paris education might work. The French school chosen was owned by Princess Mestchersky, and at the end of her first term Lord Queenborough could not believe his eyes when he received a report that his daughter was proving herself an exemplary student, co-operative and most anxious to please. Even better, he learned that she had decided to spend her holidays with the Princess, and would not be returning to disrupt his household.

Princess Mestchersky was Russian by birth, and as the wife of a Tsarist nobleman, she had expected and received instant obedience from her servants and the large number of peasants living on her husband's estate. A nod, a gesture or a quiet instruction had been all that was necessary in the days before the Revolution; and subsequently, in the school for young ladies which she started in Paris, she employed the same methods. D.P. was no ordinary young lady, but when she shouted her refusal to obey the rules, the Princess, for probably the first and only time in her life, lost her temper and shouted back.

It was a short-lived conflict, for D.P. realized she had met her match, and, significantly, the ensuing years were among the happiest in her stormy life. Princess Mestchersky took the place of the mother D.P. had loved and lost, and, as is the way of children, the respect in which she held the Princess brought a new dimension to the love she now gave so readily.

It was Princess Mestchersky who introduced D.P. to the famous singing teacher Madame Ciampi, who considered that

5

the girl possessed great potentialities if she would work hard for the next five years. Dorothy made progress with her singing, and on her return to England, continued her studies under Madame Bentham and the popular Olga Lynn. But predictably she lacked the concentration necessary to fulfil her early promise, and the only two public appearances she made which I have been able to track were at Wormwood Scrubs prison, where she sang to five hundred inmates, and at the American Women's Club in Grosvenor Street, London. In October 1924, when she was nineteen, the music correspondent of the *Evening Standard* described her as 'a dramatic soprano of more than usual merit'. He went on to say that the role of Senta in Wagner's *Flying Dutchman* was a very ambitious one for so young a singer, but that she had proved herself to be equal to it. Her accompanist was an up-and-coming young Welshman, Ivor Novello.

While D.P. was at her Paris school Princess Mestchersky started a Russian Home for elderly refugees from the Revolution. D.P. threw herself heart and soul into the project, demonstrating a compassion for those in need which remained with her throughout her life, but which she succeeded in concealing from the outside world. It was shortly after the opening of the Russian Home that D.P. met Princess Mestchersky's sister Madame Orloff. These sisters must have been remarkable characters for they engendered in D.P. a love and a sense of responsibility for her fellow human beings. Very soon Madame Orloff too became a close friend, and she accompanied D.P. when she went to the United States to visit her trustees. It was typical of her that she told only the two sisters the reason for her visit – she was still a minor and needed money for the Russian Home. For the next fifteen years D.P. supported the home single-handed, and her association with it ended only when the Germans occupied Paris in the Second World War. Madame Orloff became her paid companion and remained with her until her death. Several times a year D.P., with Madame Orloff, would slip away from her home in England on a visit to Paris – mystifying her acquaintances for she had no interest in clothes, seldom if ever visited a hairdresser, despised cosmetics, and had no cultural activities. No more than two or three people know of her association with the Russian Home and they were sworn to secrecy; she was busily occupied putting her plans into practice and as soon as her money was made available she started building.

The Home was situated at Sainte-Geneviève des Bois, and was finished in 1927. It at first took forty elderly ladies and gentlemen, but in a few years D.P. was housing two hundred refugees of all ages in a home that was entirely free providing for every need, including clothing. In the company of these people D.P. was neither awkward nor shy, and they worshipped her.

Then came the war; in 1939 a fund was organized to provide what D.P. had every reason to believe would be adequate support for as long as the war lasted, but the money was exhausted by the end of 1941. There was no possibility of arranging for further funds and the old people suffered greatly; there were no more Christmas trees, no more evening parties with Russian music, and above all the refugees felt that they had lost their only friend and benefactor. The end of the Russian Home affected her deeply, and as a result she became more remote and less accessible to her relations and friends.

A friend who was living in Paris during the thirties and frequently visited Sainte-Geneviève des Bois paid her this tribute: 'She gave unsparingly to all those in need, with an emphasis on the aged and infirm.'

2

An unusual debutante

Back in England, at the end of her schooling, D.P. drifted back into the habits of her pre-Paris days. She showed a blithe disregard for the inconvenience she caused by her almost obsessive unpunctuality and lack of awareness of the feelings of others. No longer a spoiled child, she was becoming an unconventional adult, in embryo the eccentric into which she would develop in later years.

Yet, to most outward appearances, she had emerged as just another debutante, attractive without being lovely, and with very good legs. She was no conversationalist, but, in this respect, was no different from the other debs of her time. One reporter, in 1924, described her as slim and fair haired. She may have dyed her hair, or it may have been a case of mistaken identity, for though slim she certainly was, in all her photographs she was a brunette.

Appearances were misleading, for D.P. was no ordinary deb. In particular, she scorned the traditional goal of all debs, marriage. This was despite the efforts of her elder sister Olive who, with her husband, had bought Leeds Castle and now turned her attentions to solving D.P.'s problems. She did all in her power to arrange a marriage, but D.P. actively discouraged all suitors, and though she danced at private parties, and occasionally in restaurants, it was plain that she derived no pleasure from it. Sometimes she would simply disengage herself from her partner without comment and walk off the floor, leaving the poor young man stranded and wondering what he had done wrong.

There were many suitors. Attractive, with regular features and a shy smile, the fact that she was England's greatest heiress ensured her a welcome in stately homes throughout the country. The landed gentry, who were not quite as rich as they had been prior to 1914, cast covetous eyes on her and wished that one day she might become their daughter-in-law.

As D.P. rejected son after son of some of England's noblest families, the parents of other suitors rubbed their hands as a succession of potential rivals were eliminated from the race, much as the owner of a fancied horse in the Derby rejoices when a formidable opponent is scratched. But when their own pride and joy found himself abandoned, as was inevitably the case, they came to regard her as a phenomenon quite outside their experience, not bound by the ordinary rules of the game. From having been overwhelmed with invitations to dance, D.P. found herself becoming increasingly short of partners, which did not worry her in the slightest. Even the most ardent young fortune-hunter, urged on by avaricious parents, dared not risk a third shaming, having twice been left high and dry. Among the majority it was once bitten, twice shy.

D.P.'s behaviour on ballroom floors, now the talk of Mayfair, was the direct result of her aversion to the close proximity of men and her suspicion that she was not like other girls. It was a suspicion which became a certainty before the end of her season as a debutante, though there is no evidence that it depressed her unduly. Indeed, there can be little doubt that she had considerable satisfaction in humiliating some young man who was obviously deriving physical pleasure from placing his right arm around her slim waist and clasping her to his stiff white shirt-front.

Most debs and their opposite numbers, the 'debs' delights', were snobs in those days, and D.P., in her perverse way, was no exception: it was said of her that the nobler the family,

B

the greater the thrill from leaving its son and heir stranded and blushing to the roots of his short-back-and-sides. When her own family protested at her shameful treatment of some suitor she would reply that he was only after her for her money. I never met any young man who admitted having been in love with D.P.; but then no man, young or old, is very keen to admit that he was once the object of derision.

At the end of the season someone suggested that a club should be started for young men who had been stood up or left stranded by D.P., but so far as I know it never materialized. By the time she reached her twenty-first birthday she had given up dancing altogether and had become instead a keen player of card games, on her way to developing into a compulsive gambler.

There is absolutely no proof for the widespread belief that D.P. became a man-hater as the result of having been jilted in her youth. To her death she remained aloof and it is no exaggeration to say that she was allergic to men, including her father. Perhaps fortunately, she had no brothers. She once told her cousin, May Snow, that the worst experience of her life was being kissed by a slightly tipsy middle-aged Frenchman in Claridge's Hotel in the Champs Elysées, 'I rushed to the loo and threw up,' she related.

D.P.'s only close male friend was Francis Cassel, and he was no more attracted to women than D.P. was to men. Theirs was a long-lasting friendship based, I think, on the mutual recognition that they were 'different'. He was a man of culture, while in the last thirty years of her life D.P. had no outside interests other than horse-racing, show jumping and Wimbledon tennis. Indeed, except when she went on long holidays to Germany, she displayed little enthusiasm for anything else.

Those who knew Francis Cassel have described him as a man of charm and intelligence. He was certainly not dazzled by her wealth, as he was richer than she was, but he was quite content to fetch and carry for her and to execute some of her commissions with the bookmakers. Much of her betting was done with William Hill and Ladbrokes, to whom she must have been a gold-mine, but her bets were spread over a wide range. She always settled on the nail, and betting in huge sums as she did in unimportant races on which the market was weak, it was inevitable that more often than not she took under the odds.

In this formative period of her life D.P.'s relations with her family grew no better, but deteriorated still further. She had not long returned from Paris when she had a blazing row with her father. She was very keen on hunting, and was an accomplished horsewoman, having ridden in numerous horse shows with a certain degree of success and in a number of point-to-points, though there is no record of her having won any. On this occasion it was her intention to take a hunting box in Warwickshire, but for once in his life Lord Queenborough put his foot down because, he said, it was not ladylike for a girl of her tender years. For a long time they did not speak to one another, and the first occasion on which they were seen again together was when Golden Miller won the Grand National in 1934.

Lord Queenborough's second marriage was to yet another American heiress, Edith, the daughter of millionaire William Starr Miller of New York, by whom he had three daughters. There was little love lost between D.P. and her stepmother, who died in 1933. In fact the only member of her family for whom D.P. had much time was her cousin May Paget, a charming woman who subsequently married Donald Snow, the trainer of D.P.'s flat race horses for several years from 1935.

With May as her companion D.P. took a furnished house in Bryanston Square and the following year another furnished house in Balfour Place, where she lived until 1939. She had now come of age and was able to do exactly as she liked: May described the D.P. of the mid-twenties as moody, disinclined to meet strangers, but very kind-hearted and an agreeable companion. Her singing career had stopped and she seemed rather ashamed to have once indulged in so cultural an activity. She took pleasure in her rides in Rotten Row, although it is doubtful her groom was so enthusiastic: on one occasion she ordered her horse to be ready, saddled, and at her door at 3 p.m.; but it was not until 8 p.m. that she appeared and mounted without a word of apology to the unfortunate man.

Like all spoilt children D.P. was constantly on the lookout for a new toy, and she found one in the motor-car. She had become bitten by the motor-racing bug when she went to Brooklands for the great 500-mile race in 1929 and met that delightful character and superb driver of racing cars, Tim Birkin. Earlier that year Tim, with his great friend 'Babe' Barnato, had won the Le Mans twenty-four hour endurance test. Britain's motor-racing fortunes were low from lack of funds and D.P. came to the rescue, as she was to rescue steeplechasing on an even larger scale.

Tim had a private stable of cars in Hertfordshire, and early in 1930 D.P. bought his three Bentleys which had been so successful the previous year, together with a new mystery car which was still under construction. The *Daily Express* motoring correspondent described her action as public-spirited, ensuring as it did that Britain would make a good showing in every part of the world that year.

Her venture into motor-racing started promisingly; in April 1930 one of her Bentleys, driven by Tim, broke the track record at Brooklands. Under Tim's instruction D.P. had become an enthusiastic driver, often of her own racing cars in practice runs. Tim described her as one of the finest women drivers of fast cars he had ever come across, capable of handling any make of racing car produced in this country or abroad. She was a passenger when Tim lapped at an average speed of eighty mph at Phoenix Park, Dublin, and Harold Pemberton wrote in the *Daily Express* that Birkin's cornering was dazzling. D.P. told Pemberton that she had never been so thrilled, adding, 'I must do a lot more of it.'

But D.P.'s enthusiasm for motor-racing soon waned, and in October the same year it was announced that 'The Honourable Dorothy Paget, the only woman owner of a team of racing cars, is retiring from motor-racing. Luck has been against her and her cars have failed to win a major event.' Including the cost of the cars, her one-year venture into motor-racing had entailed an outlay of over £40,000 – a mere flea-bite compared to what horse-racing was to cost her. But it was not failure which deterred her: motor-racing bored her because she could not bet on it.

Although she was only in her middle twenties D.P. was already a hardened gambler and she set the Mayfair tongues wagging again when she won £1,160 in one bank at *chemin de fer* at what was described as 'a very exclusive party'. This snob party – you had to be a member of 'exclusive social circles' even to get a ticket – was given ostensibly in aid of the Great Northern Hospital, and the Duchess of Sutherland explained to the newspapers that five per cent of all bets were devoted to the charity after deduction of 'necessary expenses'. The hospital, however, may not have benefited by as much as might have been thought, for according to the *Daily Express* 'champagne, whisky and even plebian beer were on the house'.

Stories about D.P. are legion; many of them true, some half-truths, others fabrications. The fact that most of them are detrimental to her was the result of her seeming desire to present the worst possible picture of herself to the public whom she affected to despise. She could be infuriating, and Fulke Walwyn, who trained for her with brilliant success, summed her up in the following words: 'She would drive you bloody demented, but the next moment she would say something endearing, and you would forgive her. You may not believe me but that woman had a lot of charm.' All her trainers, and she had a large number, agreed that she knew racing, that they were never kept waiting for their training fees and that she was a wonderful loser.

3

Some bad investments

For the first year or so after her return to England D.P. had taken a great deal of trouble over her appearance, but following her first full season she became less and less interested in how she looked, and long before she was out of her twenties it seemed that she went to great lengths to make herself as unattractive as possible. To her few intimate friends she would make jokes about her appearance and the fact that she was putting on weight. May Snow tells of an occasion when she, Gwendoline Foster (who, as Gwendoline Brogden, had been a very successful revue actress in the First World War) and D.P. were setting off for a racecourse. D.P. looked critically at her two companions and announced, 'Gwen is overdressed, May looks the bottom and I'm just right.' Many of her statements were made with her tongue in her cheek, and even those nearest to her were never quite sure when she wanted to be taken seriously.

But if her appearance meant little to her, her horses meant a great deal, for it was now that she began to develop that life-long passion for the Turf which was to cost her millions of pounds and keep her so much in the public eye that she became, apart from royalty, the best-known woman in the land.

In fact, despite the scale of her racecourse activities, she started her career as an owner by accident. She used to hunt regularly during the winter months and one day a hunter called Bridget ran away with her; so she sent the animal to be trained at Findon by Alec Law, a shrewd man who trained many winners. He duly won a race with Bridget, but he had only a small stable: D.P. decided in typical fashion that she would indulge her new hobby in the grand manner and that her trainer must be prepared to train at least fifty horses. Accordingly, she appointed Basil Briscoe, an old Etonian not long down from Cambridge, as her trainer both on the flat and over the jumps. Unkind people have expressed the view that it was snobbishness which dictated her choice of a young member of a distinguished family in preference to one of the old-time professionals.

Briscoe, however, had been well grounded in the racing business by that great trainer and lovable character 'Jack' Leader. He had already turned out a number of winners for Mr Philip Carr and other wealthy owners, and had ridden with some success in point-to-points and races for amateur riders. A young man of charm and a sense of humour, he loved nothing more than for his many friends to share in his 'good things', or perhaps I should say his supposedly good things, as Basil was a great optimist. This generosity sometimes led to high words between D.P. and himself when she pointed out, with some justification, that as she was the heaviest punter owning horses, they would start at short enough odds without his advertising their prospects far and wide.

In her thirty years of racehorse owning there were many stories of the huge sums she had won, but no one bothered to report the still more gigantic sums she lost. At the end of the 1931–2 season she was said to have won over £60,000 from the ring, which may well have been true as her jumpers had enjoyed spectacular success. On one occasion a reporter, obviously sadly ignorant on racing matters, announced that the Hon. Dorothy Paget had broken the Tote, but as we know to our cost the Tote always wins, no matter how much money is bet on the winner.

Basil Briscoe was training at stables he had built on his

15

father's estate at Longstow near Cambridge when D.P. informed him, in the imperious manner which was all her own, that he was to be her trainer. She did not consider it necessary to ask people to do things, believing that it would be highly unlikely that they would decline to serve England's richest woman and one who had a reputation for generosity to her employees. A few days after her horses had arrived at Longstow, Basil's telephone rang and he was told D.P. wished to speak to him. She never put through a call herself, nor answered the telephone, but having picked up the receiver she would talk for hours if she felt like it. On this occasion her orders were short and to the point – 'buy the Waffles colt'. Sandwich, by Sansovino out of Waffles, had already scored some successes that year and his half-brother, by Derby winner Spion Kop, would surely fetch a huge sum. Sandwich was not the only distinguished son of Waffles, her son Manna by Phalaris having won the Two Thousand Guineas and the Derby six years earlier.

Realizing that many of the leading owners would be bidding for a colt of such illustrious parentage, Basil asked what her limit was. 'Don't ask bloody silly questions. I said buy him,' she replied, and replaced the receiver. The following day the Waffles colt was knocked down to Basil Briscoe for 6,600 guineas; it was not to prove one of her more fortunate purchases.

D.P. gave the name Tuppence to the son of Spion Kop and Waffles, and that sum turned out to be far nearer his true value than the 6,600 guineas she had paid for him. We all know what may happen to a dog if we give him a bad name, and I have found that horses given foolish names seldom make good. Tuppence was no exception: his first contribution towards D.P.'s outlay was £53 as a result of dead-heating in a race at Hamilton Park, while his total earnings amounted to approximately £500. Yet with the cost of keeping him in training, plus entries and forfeits, Tuppence must have cost her the best part of £10,000.

D.P. was one of the most superstitious women who ever

16

set foot on a racecourse, and one would have expected her to believe that it was asking for trouble to select so unpropitious a name as Tuppence for a horse she hoped might win the Derby. Still, although Tuppence had not a million to one chance D.P. was determined to run him in the 1933 Derby against her trainer's advice, for she wanted to see her colours carried in the greatest race of all.

Five days before the race Tuppence was freely on offer at 250–1, but all of a sudden money was poured on him all over the country, not in large sums but in sufficient volume for the bookmakers to cut his price from 250–1 to 100–1. Still the money flowed into the bookmakers' offices for Tuppence, and continued to do so until the horses were actually at the post. The bookmakers stood to lose millions, and Tuppence's price was finally cut to 10–1, at which he started fourth favourite. He was never seen with a chance, and finished third from last, the winner being Lord Derby's mighty little horse Hyperion, who went on to win the St Leger.

All sorts of stories were circulated as to the source of the information which resulted in thousands of punters putting their money on Tuppence. A popular theory was that D.P. had dreamt he would win and placed a large bet on him, but I refuse to accept that story. D.P. was not a particularly shrewd backer of horses, but she had a thorough understanding of the animals and racing, and she would not have bet really heavily on a horse which she and her trainer knew had no earthly chance, even had she dreamt it would win every night for a week.

I think the most likely explanation is that the tip for Tuppence was circulated by unscrupulous bookmakers who, realizing the colt had no chance, spread the rumour that they had laid him to lose thousands. Rumours of inspired money invariably attract the mug punters and the ruse enriched the whole bookmaking fraternity by millions, because, although the Derby was won by the favourite, few if any bookmakers lost money on the race.

Tuppence was eventually put to jumping, until when

contesting a hurdle race of £100 at Huntingdon he ran out at a flight of hurdles, dashed into the crowd and fatally injured a spectator. D.P. was very distressed at this accident and she was glad to see the back of him when he eventually won a selling race. He ended his days in Poland. So far as I know no one has subsequently called a racehorse Tuppence, and having read this story I doubt whether anyone will do so again.

Another disastrous purchase was a daughter of Fairway, whom D.P. named Osway, and who cost 8,000 guineas. Briscoe could do nothing with her, she was so temperamental, but excitable animals will sober down in the company of a sheep or a goat and Basil bought a goat to keep Osway company. She took a great fancy to him, but though she mended her manners she did not run any faster and failed to win a race of any sort.

An even greater failure in the D.P. colours was Colonel Payne, so called for no better reason than she had a relative of that name. It was ironical that the horse which cost D.P. a fortune was named after the man who contributed substantially to her great wealth: D.P.'s grandfather, W. C. Whitney, married Flora, a daughter of Henry B. Payne, one of the founders of Standard Oil, and Colonel Payne was Whitney's brother-in-law. In due course the Colonel inherited the Payne millions, and when he died a bachelor his money went into the Whitney pool.

Most owners take infinite trouble in finding appropriate names for their horses, but not D.P. – In fact she seldom bothered to name them until they were three years old, a practice no longer permitted. Colonel Payne was by Fairway out of Golden Hair, and was therefore a half-brother to Orwell, one of the best two-year-olds to run between the wars, and the winner as a three-year-old of the Greenham Stakes and the Two Thousand Guineas, for which he started at even money. He finished unplaced in the Derby and St Leger as he did not stay further than a mile.

When D.P. learned that Orwell's half-brother was coming

up for sale she was determined to buy him, and she did so at the cost of 15,000 guineas and sent him to Frank Butters, but when he failed to win a race in two seasons she decided he must be trained by Fred Darling at Beckhampton. Not only was Fred one of the greatest trainers, he was also one of the most autocratic, and his owners had to toe the line. We have already seen that Princess Mestchersky was the only person to whose wishes D.P. had deferred, so it was a certainty that it would not be long before the storm broke.

Colonel Payne had taken time to come to hand, and a knee injury preventing him running as a three-year-old, but in the early summer of his four-year-old career he revealed brilliant speed in a home gallop and Fred Darling thought he was certain to win the Cork and Orrery Stakes at Ascot, in which he would be ridden by Gordon Richards.

Fred told D.P. to put her shirt on him, and in consequence she had the biggest bet of her life; I understand that her first bet was one of £10,000 and that she went on backing him until the horses were at the post. But even the greatest trainer in the world cannot guarantee that a horse will reproduce his home form when he takes part in a race (though fortunately the majority of horses do). Colonel Payne, alas, was what is known among the racing fraternity as a Morning Glory, so called because home gallops take place before breakfast while races are held after lunch. Morning Glories are also referred to by other names among disgruntled punters, and that day at Ascot Colonel Payne merited all the abuse that was hurled at him for, having declined to take hold of his bit at any stage of the race, he finished nearer last than first.

For so large a woman – and D.P. had put on a lot of weight in recent years – she could move at great speed. None of the female secretaries she always had in tow could keep up with her, and I always kept well clear of her, realizing that a man of less than average size might receive nasty injuries in the event of a head-on collision. Having covered the distance from the Royal Enclosure to the paddock in record

19

time, she interrogated Gordon Richards as he dismounted. 'Where's Mr Darling?' she demanded, repeating the question several times in the staccato tones she used when she was agitated.

On the ground, Gordon barely came up to her ample bosom, but he fixed her with steadfast brown eyes and replied, 'I wouldn't be quite sure, Miss Paget, but I've a pretty shrewd idea he's on the top of the stand cutting his throat.' This was a reply after D.P.'s own heart, and though she had lost an astronomical sum she burst out laughing. From that moment the two became firm friends, though her association with Fred Darling only lasted a few more weeks.

In the years to come Gordon rode many winners in D.P.'s blue and yellow colours, and when the twenty-six times champion jockey, now Sir Gordon, retired from the saddle in 1954, she asked him to become her trainer. They never exchanged a cross word and he was still training for her at the time of her death.

4

Two great horses

Very early in her career as an owner D.P. hoped to bring off the Lincoln–Grand National Double (a feat which, over forty years later, has still to be accomplished) with Breadcrumb and Solanum. Breadcrumb unfortunately went lame a few days before the race and could not run, and Solanum fell while leading at Bechers, second time round. It was typical of her luck. But D.P. continued to pay huge prices for yearlings, and for the second year running outbid the Aga Khan and Lord Glanely by giving 5,000 guineas for Portrait, a colt by Tetratema. In the autumn of 1933, however, she went into the bloodstock market in a bigger way than ever. By now, part of her outlay was directed at fillies and brood mares, with the intention of breeding her own racehorses instead of buying them at the yearling sales. Three of the highest prices she paid were 6,200 guineas for Dorigen, 6,000 guineas for Speckle and 8,200 guineas for Salome.

By this time D.P.'s stable included two horses which were to achieve immortality. Indeed, when she made her original choice of Basil Briscoe as her trainer she had undoubtedly been influenced by the fact that he was training Insurance and Golden Miller – respectively the most promising hurdler and steeplechaser seen in Britain for a long time. Briscoe had been training them for Mr Philip Carr, a great sportsman and a wonderful judge of horses, but Carr was in failing health, and when, towards the end of 1931, D.P.

learned that he might be prepared to sell them she offered £12,000 for the pair. The offer was accepted. This may not seem a great deal of money today, but it was a very big price for National Hunt horses forty years ago, and the only chance she had of getting her money back was if one of them won the Grand National.

Basil Briscoe himself had briefly owned Golden Miller in 1930. In March of that year he had received a telegram from Ireland from a Captain Farmer, who was a partner of John Drage, the well-known Northamptonshire horse-dealer, offering him an unbroken three-year-old out of Miller's Pride for £500. Basil had trained two useful horses out of the mare, so he wired back 'Yes, sending cheque.' A week later the horse arrived, and when Basil saw him he cursed himself for being a mug and buying a horse he had never seen.

The three-year-old had been running in a field all his life and his previous owner had not bothered to scrape the mud off him before sending him to England. Weary after his long journey by sea and rail, the animal stood in his box with his head down, looking the soul of dejection. In due course, having been cleaned and clipped (his coat under the mud was found to be several inches long), he was broken in. He gave no trouble, but appeared apathetic. Such horses seldom do much, and when Basil told his head lad that he'd named the animal Golden Miller, he received the reply, 'that's too good a name for a bad horse.'

After he had been ridden for several weeks Basil entered Golden Miller in a maiden three-year-old race at Southwell, where he ran abominably, apparently taking no interest in the proceedings, his slovenly attitude suggesting that he was useless. To awaken in him some interest in life, Basil rode him out hunting with the Fitzwilliam Hounds, on one of those days hunting men dream about, when hounds seem to be running all day. But poor Basil had the most uncomfortable time of his life: not only did Golden Miller seem unable to negotiate the simplest obstacle, but he was so slow he could not keep within hail of the hounds. To add injury to insult, he was found to be lame the following morning, no doubt the result of taking every fence by the roots.

Mr Carr, however, saw potentialities in this apparently useless horse, and offered Briscoe £1,000 for him. Basil, who could hardly believe his luck at being offered twice the sum he had given for him, eagerly accepted the offer.

Mr Carr's judgement was not long in being vindicated. Soon after he had bought him he ran Golden Miller in an all-age hurdle race at Newbury and, the only three-year-old in the field, he delighted his new owner by finishing third. His rider, Bob Lyall, a leading National Hunt jockey, described him as one of the most promising three-year-olds he had ever ridden.

Golden Miller had always been a lovable horse, with his placid ways, and now he was developing into a magnificent-looking animal. His next two races at Leicester and Nottingham were won by wide margins, and from then on he went from strength to strength, so that by the time D.P. became his owner his name was a household word.

Insurance, the horse D.P. had bought along with Golden Miller, soon proved himself the best hurdler since the immortal Trespasser. D.P. was on the crest of the wave and certainly deserved her change of luck. Up till that time her ventures in both motor-racing and horse-racing had cost her a fortune by almost anyone else's standards, and she had received scant reward. When, following one of her many defeats, she was described as the world's best loser she remarked ruefully, 'I ought to be. I've had plenty of practice.' Now she was winning, though despite landing some huge bets, the prize money could be described only as peanuts.

Her greatest triumph to date came at Cheltenham in 1932, when Insurance won the Champion Hurdle and Golden Miller the Gold Cup on the same day, victories which brought her in a total of £1,340. Both races were what are known as £1,000 plates, out of which the winner received £670, the remaining £330 being divided between the second and third. Golden Miller and Insurance won the same two races the following year and Insurance was strongly fancied to win the Grand Course de Haies (the French champion hurdle) at Auteuil. D.P. and her entourage went to Paris with high hopes of success, but Insurance was a bad traveller and the sea crossing so upset him that he finished nearly last.

When Golden Miller, as a five-year-old, took on the best steeplechase horses in the country in the Cheltenham Gold Cup for the first time, it was only three and a half months after he had made his debut as a steeplechaser and many good judges thought that D.P. was aiming too high with so inexperienced a horse. They forecast that he would be ruined as the result of taking on the best over the most testing 3¼-mile course in the country. After all, a number of horses who have won the 4½-mile Grand National have failed to stay the course at Cheltenham. However D.P.'s faith in the youthful Golden Miller was vindicated up to the hilt when he stormed to victory at 13–2 (the bookmakers were not so generous when he won the Gold Cup on four subsequent occasions). Golden Miller was of course still too immature for the Grand National, but it was decided to run him in the Lancashire Chase at Manchester despite the fact that he was set to carry a 12 lb penalty. He was probably a little stale at the end of a hard season, and he could finish only fourth.

D.P. had already taken Golden Miller to her heart, and though she had never been known to display any emotion in public she is described in the *Daily Express* on one occasion as 'dashing from the members' stand and displaying a fleetness of foot which defied her companions to match. She greeted him at the paddock with three endearing kisses.' A cynical onlooker was heard to say that it was the first time that she had ever kissed a member of the opposite sex. 'And he's a gelding,' his even more cynical companion replied.

During Golden Miller's 1932–3 season, when his first race was on 1 December and his sixth and final one the Grand National, the horse was winner of the first five, proving himself the greatest steeplechaser of all time, though he was still only six years old. He was already a wonderful weight carrier and early in February carried 12.10 to victory in the Troytrown Handicap Chase at Lingfield. D.P. was in the seventh heaven of delight. She had already begun to turn night into day, and often did not rise from her bed until after dark; but she was always up in time to see Golden Miller go to post, though she sometimes cut matters very fine.

In the Grand National Golden Miller was going like a winner passing the stand first time round but he blundered at Bechers second time round, and made such a bad mistake at the Canal Turn that he unseated Ted Leader, the greatest jockey of his day round Aintree. Leader had won the 1931 Gold Cup on Golden Miller, but in the horse's five victories in 1932-3 he was ridden by Billy Scott because Leader was riding as first jockey for his father and was not always available.

Great horse though he had proved himself to be in 1932-3, Golden Miller's most memorable year came in the following season. In March 1934 he won the Gold Cup at Cheltenham, and, seventeen days later, the Grand National at Aintree; a feat which had never been accomplished before and, I feel sure, never will be again. Gerry Wilson had been engaged to ride him in all these races; though he was twice beaten in the course of that season, it transpired that he was taking on impossible tasks in conceding weight to horses who subsequently proved themselves very high-class chasers indeed. Golden Miller won the Gold Cup by six lengths from a very good horse, Avenger, with Kellsboro Jack, winner of the previous year's Grand National, eight lengths away in third place.

And now for his greatest task of all – the Grand National.

By this time D.P. owned so many horses that Basil Briscoe moved from his stables at Longstowe to the more spacious Beechwood House stable at Exning on the outskirts of Newmarket. Here Briscoe gave him a few days' rest and then,

25

C

meticulously, sharpened him up so that he was in the peak of condition when he left Newmarket for Liverpool. One of the most placid horses that ever lived, nothing worried Golden Miller, who reserved all his energy for the racecourse and was endowed, too, with a wonderful physique. But writing as one who was privileged to witness all his great triumphs, I think his outstanding quality was his almost human intelligence. He was the most economical jumper I ever saw, in that he knew exactly how much energy he had to expend at every fence, and I never saw Golden Miller clear a fence, big or small, with more than a few inches to spare. Although on three occasions at Liverpool he hit fences sufficiently hard to unseat his riders, he himself never fell.

On that great day, however, in March 1934 he did everything perfectly. He was carrying 12.2, a big weight round Liverpool, and he was only seven years old. D.P. and her trainer both had a fortune on him, and as everybody I met that day seemed to have backed him it was remarkable that he started at odds as long as 8–1.

The visibility, for once, was excellent and Golden Miller, who was up with the leaders all the way, never appeared to put a foot wrong. With just under a mile to go Delaneige, the 1932 winner Forbra, Thomond II and Golden Miller had the race between them. Delaneige led Golden Miller over the last fence, but the Miller was going twice as well, and when Gerry Wilson asked him for an effort on the flat he sprinted away to win by five lengths. He had beaten the course record by no fewer than eight seconds!

I have never witnessed such a scene on a racecourse. The huge crowd went mad, and no other woman owner would have been able to fight her way through that dense, cheering, dancing throng and seize Golden Miller's rein and lead him in. This was, I am certain, the greatest moment in D.P.'s life, made all the more wonderful by the disappointments which had preceded it. The most composed character at Aintree, as Gerry Wilson unsaddled, was the hero himself, who appeared utterly unconcerned as the souvenir hunters pulled hairs from his tail.

No horse in the history of the Turf had achieved such popularity and whenever he appeared on a racecourse there was always a big welcoming crowd, so he was certainly a wonderful asset to hard-pressed racecourse executives. At Cheltenham they had to close the gates, something which had never happened before.

It was typical of 'unpredictable Dorothy', as she had come to be known, that having paid upwards of £100,000 for blood stock, and seen her beloved Golden Miller earn immortality, she should disappear without trace. But when month succeeded month and there was still no sign of her, the curiosity of the racing community was aroused. All sorts of rumours were circulated, one of the least likely to reach my ears being that she had married and was living on a desert island. In fact, she was spending a small fortune on telephone calls to her trainer, demanding to be told every detail of her horses' progress: Basil assured her that Golden Miller was better than ever and he was sure the horse would win the Grand National for the second year running, despite having five more pounds to carry.

D.P. would carry on a telephone conversation for an hour or more, and was just as domineering over the phone as she was in the flesh. In the nine months she was away she frequently caused her trainer consternation by entering horses for races on her own account without telling him what she had done. From her telephone calls Basil Briscoe knew she was living in Germany, but training bills were dealt with by her secretary and he did not know her address. She was now reconciled with her father, and he and her sister, Lady Baillie, were probably in her confidence, though they were never a close-knit family.

On her return, D.P. declined to discuss her movements during the past months and a newspaper reporter who was intrepid enough to question her was told to mind his own business. Nearly forty years later I am able to disclose that she spent the entire time in idyllic surroundings on the banks of the Rhine in a small village near Wiesbaden.

Her hosts were the de Mumm family. Madame de Mumm was a sister of Princess Mestchersky, who had exercised such a beneficial influence on her in Paris ten years earlier. Madame de Mumm's daughter Olili, was still living with her parents, and although Golden Miller came first in D.P.'s life at that time the beautiful Olili ran him a close second.

In Olili's company, D.P. was a different person for the simple reason that Olili was the only human being for whom she had real love. She grew quite fond of those women who served her over the years, but it was no more than an easy tolerance, and she was often highly critical of them. In the presence of Olili however she was undemanding and gentle, her imperious manner giving way to one of sweet reason, and only when she picked up the receiver to talk to her trainer did the old D.P. reassert herself.

Golden Miller had won his four races prior to going to Cheltenham for his fourth Gold Cup in great style, but because Briscoe felt that the Gold Cup would require very little winning he had been easy with him so that he would benefit from the race and be at concert pitch for the Grand National. A few days before the race, however, D.P.'s cousin Jock Whitney decided to run Thomond II, who by this time was a very good horse indeed. The result was that a three parts fit Golden Miller had a desperately hard race.

In the greatest finish for a steeplechase I have ever seen Golden Miller's great courage was the deciding factor, and he won by three-quarters of a length after these two gallant horses had jumped the last six fences stride for stride. But for the first time in his career Golden Miller was distressed at the end of the race. D.P. always led Golden Miller in after his victories, and on this occasion she was described in a newspaper report as taking longer strides than Golden Miller. She nearly missed seeing that great victory, having left Frankfurt by private aircraft that morning, changed

28

planes at Croydon, and arriving only a few minutes before the race.

Golden Miller looked bright enough when he went to post for the Grand National and Basil Briscoe told me that when he had arrived at Aintree the Miller had cleaned out his manger, lain down and gone fast asleep. He appeared to me to be jumping as cleanly and cleverly as in the previous year, as he sailed over Bechers, the Canal Turn and Valentine's, but at the fence after Valentine's he parted company with his rider, Gerry Wilson.

That fence is admittedly a long way from the stands, but I had my binoculars focused on him at the time and it seemed to me that if the Miller made a mistake it was only a very slight one. Wilson's explanation was that Golden Miller had gone short cantering to post, and when going to the fence after Valentine's he propped and went lame. He added, 'he did not fall but shot me out of the saddle.' Those nearer the fence shared my view, and never has the exit of a horse in the Grand National created such a sensation. Golden Miller had started a red-hot favourite, and all sorts of rumours were circulated, one of the most widespread being that Gerry Wilson was in the pay of the bookmakers and had thrown himself off.

This, I hardly need say, was arrant nonsense, but I have always held the view that, perhaps through over-confidence in the horse which had carried him to victory the previous year, Wilson was not gripping as tightly as he should have done, and when Golden Miller made a trifling mistake he fell off.

I do not pretend to know what passed between D.P., her trainer and jockey at the subsequent post-mortem, but months later, Briscoe told me that D.P. accepted Gerry Wilson's explanation. A flaming row ensued between her and Basil and he asked her to remove her horses from his stable.

D.P.'s horses went to be trained by Donald Snow at Eastbury, and Golden Miller and the jumpers were subsequently sent to Owen Anthony's stables. Owen, a brother of Jack

Anthony who won the Grand National three times as a jockey and subsequently trained Jock Whitney's Easter Hero (the greatest horse who ran in the Grand National, but never won it) was a genial, likeable man with only a small stable. He was able to devote his wealth of experience with horses to restoring Golden Miller's confidence, and, having succeeded in this in late December, Golden Miller, ridden by Gerry Wilson, won the Andover Chase at Newbury carrying 12.10 over two miles. He was an extremely versatile horse and was almost as effective over two miles as he was over 3¼ miles. He loved Cheltenham, and, ridden by Evan Williams, he won the Gold Cup for the fifth time, beating by twelve lengths Royal Mail, who was to win the Grand National the following year under 11.13.

Golden Miller went to post for two more Grand Nationals, but he made it quite clear in 1936 that he now hated the sight of Aintree, and I cannot imagine what induced D.P. to run him again in 1937. In 1936 he refused at the first fence, and in 1937 he got as far as the twelfth obstacle when he refused again.

One might have thought that five Gold Cups would have satisfied D.P., but she derived so much delight from seeing him in action over his favourite course that she decided that he should try and win it for the sixth time, despite the fact that he had shown signs that he was not quite the horse he was. There is nothing so pathetic as the evening of a great reputation, and I was only one of thousands who brushed away a tear when he was fairly and squarely beaten. The winner, Morse Code, was a good horse, but the Miller in his heyday would have picked him up and carried him.

In his career, extending over seven seasons, Golden Miller won thirty-one races valued at £15,176. His first two successes were worth £83 and £88 respectively, none of his five Gold Cups was worth more than £670 to the winner, while his victory in the Grand National brought in £7,265. Had he been born thirty-five years later I reckon his earnings would have been somewhere between £150,000 and £200,000.

Who was the greater – Golden Miller or Arkle? Arkle was the more spectacular and when on several occasions he treated Mill House, a previous winner of the Gold Cup (and, until the appearance of Arkle, regarded as the best chaser since the Miller), as if he were a selling plater, he performed feats which, in my view, would have proved beyond the powers of Golden Miller. On the other hand, Golden Miller won the Gold Cup five times against Arkle's three, and seventeen days after winning his third Gold Cup he won the Grand National under 12.2 in record time.

Arkle never appealed to me as a National horse, though the race has been won by horses of all shapes and sizes. However, the Duchess of Westminster must have shared my view, as she never entered Arkle at Liverpool.

Both horses made Turf history and were largely responsible for jumping now being every bit as popular as flat racing. So does it really matter which was the greater? A champion can only beat those who were around at the same time as himself.

The Miller was the kindest and most friendly of horses, in fact he was positively gregarious. In his greatest years, when he was trained by Basil Briscoe, he and Basil's huge Great Dane, Grouse, became bosom friends, and Grouse would spend hours in his box with him. When the Miller left the stables for a race meeting Grouse would watch him being boxed, and would greet him, barking joyfully, on his return, and in the absence of his friend, Grouse would never enter the Miller's box. On the day Golden Miller was led away for the last time Grouse slunk away with his tail between his legs and lay down on the straw in the Miller's empty box. He was inconsolable, and for days refused to eat.

Golden Miller and Insurance had only been casual acquaintances during their racing days, but when these two immortals were retired to spend their remaining days in the ease and luxury of the Elsenham stud farm in Essex they became great friends. When Insurance died it was the Miller's turn to grieve. Overcome with sorrow, he would neither eat nor respond to the overtures of those who cared for him.

31

D.P. went down to see him, and was horrified by his appearance, for it was evident that unless he could be roused from his apathy he would fade away.

D.P. was renowned for her brainwaves, many of which ended in disaster, but her belief that Golden Miller might react favourably to the company of a donkey was fulfilled. Though she could lie in bed for days on end, breakfasting at 8.30 p.m. and dining at 7.00 a.m., when the spirit moved her she could get around at an incredible speed, shouting complicated directions at her retinue of secretaries, who were ever either waiting or pursuing her to carry out her commands. Within minutes of bidding farewell to her grief-stricken horse, D.P. had heard of a very valuable Anglo-Arabian donkey which she thought might be suitable, and was travelling at high speed to 'vet' him. It was a strange-looking animal with ears twice the length of the average donkey's and its name was Aggie, short for Agapanthus. 'Just the thing. He'll make the Miller laugh,' was D.P.'s verdict, and she ordered one of her horseboxes to fetch him. When he arrived it was D.P. who introduced him to Golden Miller, and I do not know whether he actually made Golden Miller laugh, but I can assert that they became firm friends and remained so for the rest of the Miller's life.

5

God's gift to breeders

Discussion on what was now known as the Golden Miller
affair continued throughout the summer of 1935, and at Royal
Ascot people were still arguing the rights and wrongs of the
case. The consensus was that D.P. and Basil Briscoe could
not be so foolish as to end an association which had proved
so profitable to both of them, when a conciliatory word on
either side might heal the wounds. Most racing people sided
with Briscoe, whom they regarded as the underdog. The
trainer had freely stated his side of the case while D.P., as
always, had kept her own counsel.

Their love of racing apart, D.P. and Briscoe had little in
common, but it was now apparent that they were both as
obstinate as mules, and the suggestion to either party that an
olive branch would be welcomed was turned down with
scorn. Eventually, under considerable pressure, D.P. handed
the following statement to a *Daily Express* representative,
and as it was the first occasion on which she had made a
written statement to a newspaper it was quite a scoop:

It is a terrible thing for an owner when a trainer and jockey
disagree. One feels one would like to be loyal to both, but unfortunately my trainer has taken the matter into his own hands by
his recent statements. He has made his decision and clearly does
not wish to accept the grave responsibility and worry of training
a horse so much in the public eye as Golden Miller. I am more
than grateful to Mr Briscoe for all the wonderful successes and

joy he he has brought me through Golden Miller and I wish him the best of luck.

The unwitting cause of the break was D.P.'s cousin Jock Whitney. Had he not changed his mind, as, of course, he was perfectly entitled to do, and taken on Golden Miller with Thomond II in the Gold Cup, D.P.'s champion would have had an easy race and gone to post for the Grand National, fit and fresh as he had done the previous year. I am not saying he would have justified his starting price of 2–1 (surely the most absurd odds at which any horse has ever started for a steeplechase), but there could have been no suggestion that he was overtrained. A horse of Golden Miller's physique can be subjected to a very hard race and emerge unscathed if he is one hundred per cent fit, but Golden Miller was not completely fit when he contested that unforgettable race with Thomond II at Cheltenham and the ordeal undoubtedly took its toll of his resources.

D.P. was a good judge of her horses and could detect the slightest change in his appearance. She expressed the view that Golden Miller looked light when he ran at Liverpool, and in this she was perfectly right, though she was wrong in attributing it to Briscoe's having over-galloped him – Golden Miller's loss of weight and condition was the result of his severe race in the Gold Cup. The possibility of his being lame was ruled out a few hours after the race when he was examined by two eminent veterinary surgeons, who reported that the horse was absolutely sound.

With her knowledge of horses and racing it was, however, an incredible decision on D.P.'s part to run Golden Miller in the Champion Chase twenty-four hours after he had parted company with Wilson in the National. I have already referred to Golden Miller's intelligence, and this was never better exemplified than when he got rid of Wilson for the second time, this time at the first fence, without coming to any harm himself. He realized that he was over the top and in no state, physically or mentally, to tackle these huge fences, and he also knew exactly how much it would take to unseat Wilson. Only the cleverest jumper in the world could have achieved the objective, but I have never been in any doubt that Golden Miller was the cleverest horse that ever lived.

Donald Snow, who was married to D.P.'s cousin May, was training in a modest way at Eastbury when he received a call from D.P. to the effect that she was transferring all her horses trained by Briscoe at Exning to his yard in Berkshire. Donald explained that he had not boxes for half the number of horses she contemplated sending him, but D.P. replied, 'You'll take the lot or none at all,' and rang off. For the next twenty-four hours Donald and May scoured Berkshire and Wiltshire for billets for the vast influx of horses. Eventually they were all stabled, though some had to rough it in cow-sheds before Donald could rent stables at Ogbourne. It was not intended that Snow should train the jumpers, but Golden Miller remained with him until he went to be trained by Owen Anthony at Wantage in August.

It has often been said of D.P. that she was her own worst enemy, but as she courted unpopularity she cannot be commiserated with on achieving it – her hostile defence of her privacy never wavered, and a suitable epitaph would have been, 'She minded her own business, and expected everyone else to mind theirs'. She was alleged to have said that journalists were an unnecessary evil, which was inconsistent with the fact that she was never seen on the racecourse without at least half a dozen newspapers clasped to her ample bosom.

She possessed an extensive knowledge of horses and racing but did not consider herself to be a sufficiently good judge of a jumper to buy one without consulting Charlie Rogers who later ran her Irish stud farm Ballymacoll and trained most of her jumpers in that country. Her flat racehorses were chosen on their pedigrees, and were therefore certain to cost the most money.

All through her life D.P. laboured under two misfortunes – her aversion to the opposite sex and her vast wealth. The former was of course beyond her control and may have been a contributory factor to her belief that money could buy anything, and that happiness, like any other commodity, would fall to the nod of the highest bidder. I have already referred to her obstinacy, and since her only male friend was even richer than she, there was nobody to convince her otherwise.

Occasionally, when she was guilty of some more than usually outrageous statement, her number-one secretary, Miss Williams, would explain with due politeness that she was talking nonsense. Having given it her careful consideration D.P. would sometimes capitulate and with a rueful smile exclaim, 'You win.' No one, however, could ever persuade her that money has its limitations, and her conviction that she could win every race in the book, provided she was prepared to pay enough, was not shaken by an unprecedented run of failure.

Her approach to the problem of securing classic winners was amateurish in the extreme: simply having studied the sales catalogues she would place a tick against the names of those closely related to recent classic winners and instruct her agent to buy them. Short of winning an important flat race nothing gave her more pleasure than outbidding the Aga Khan, Lord Glanely or Mrs Corlette Glorney who, in the thirties, were almost as profligate as she in their expenditure. She was obsessed with the view that if a certain mating had produced a champion a repetition of it must prove equally successful.

D.P. was God's gift to breeders and, in giving what amounted to a blank cheque to her agents, she was playing into the hands of the unscrupulous. I am not suggesting that all who buy and sell horses are corrupt, but it is a big temptation for a breeder to get a friend to 'run up' his horse in the knowledge that this bid would be capped.

It was said of D.P. she could never see the horse for his pedigree, and it is a fact that several yearlings for which she paid vast sums did not please their prospective trainers by their make and shape. Frank Butters was not at all impressed with the looks and mannerisms of Radiant, a full sister to Windsor Lad, but D.P. was certain that she had inherited the ability of one of the greatest horses of all time, and instructed by D.P. to buy her at all costs, Butters had to go to £11,500 guineas to secure her. Radiant won two small races but never bred a winner, and one way and another must have cost D.P. the best part of £50,000.

Had she employed an adviser of the knowledge and integrity of Noel Murless, who would have insisted she bred and bought on scientific lines instead of automatically purchasing the most expensive horses in the catalogue, her career as an owner would have been infinitely more successful. No one can say how much she was out of pocket as the result of her career as an owner of flat racehorses, but three million pounds would seem to be a conservative estimate and that sum does not include her betting losses. From time to time she won very large sums betting, but it was not till she had her jumpers trained by Fulke Walwyn and later her flat racehorses trained by Sir Gordon Richards that she had more than the occasional winning year.

D.P. would win and lose mammoth sums without batting an eyelid, but as neither winning nor losing would make any difference to her way of living this was not greatly to her credit. Could she, just once, have experienced the joy of the not-so-rich, when by a stroke of good fortune they recoup their losses at the end of a terrifying unsuccessful Royal Ascot, how much happier her life would have been. There is no doubt, however, that she derived a thrill from betting, and after landing a big bet she would be wildly excited and distribute fivers to members of her staff.

Only once did she reveal a trace of nervousness after making a bet. I do not know the name of the horse but I do know that it was not one of hers and she had made up her mind that it was a certainty, but there was nothing very original about that as every tipster in the morning and midday papers had made it his selection and it was quoted in the betting forecasts at 2–1 on. Apparently all the omens were favourable, no one wearing green had been near her for at least a week, and she had seen a couple of magpies and the correct number of black cats. She therefore covered the horse to win her £20,000.

A few minutes before the race was due to start, the secretary on telephone duty reported to her that her bookmaker was on the line and wished to inform her that the horse was 8–1 on. Would she therefore like to cancel her bet, which entailed an outlay of £160,000? With an air of outraged dignity D.P. replied, 'Inform him I consider his question a piece of gross impertinence.' This was an example of her arrogant bravado, for she was a snob, and for a member of the lower classes to question her ability to write a cheque for £160,000 was an unforgivable insult.

Her hand was seen to shake and she wiped beads of perspiration from her forehead while she gazed transfixed at the tape machine. When the right name was tapped out on the narrow strip of paper she gave a beaming smile to the secretaries standing nearby and dealt out fivers to everyone in the vicinity. Had the horse lost her cheque would have arrived at the bookmaker's office first post on Monday morning.

This I believe to have been the biggest bet D.P. ever made, but once at Royal Ascot, Mr James Rothschild, who was as eccentric as she was and possibly even richer, laid £200,000 to £50,000 on Mannamead, a horse of Lord Astor's. Mannamead could only dead-heat at 4–1 on, so Mr Rothschild lost £75,000. Rothschild who, like D.P. died intestate, only bet occasionally; but D.P. bet in large sums every day of the week.

6

'The public don't pay my bills'

An example of the lengths to which D.P. would go to alienate herself from public esteem was her refusal to allow Golden Miller's racing plates to be auctioned for charity. It was typical of her that she then proceeded, unbeknown to anyone except her secretary, to send a large donation to the same charity, insisting that she remain anonymous.

Although she had paid large sums for all her flat racehorses, trained by Donald Snow, they turned out to be disappointing. An exception was the Bossover colt by Blenheim. Ridden by Steve Donoghue, the Bossover colt made an impressive debut when winning at York in May. Subsequently, ridden by Charlie Smirke, he won the £5,000 National Breeders Produce Stakes at Sandown, and not only was this the most valuable flat race D.P. had won so far, but she also had one of her large bets on him. Donald Snow was therefore a very popular young man that evening.

Although that race was over only five furlongs the Bossover colt had won it so impressively that the bookmakers quoted him at 6–1 for the following year's Derby, but gambler though she was, this ridiculous price did not tempt D.P. as she realized that the colt's breeding could entail stamina limitations, and so it proved to be. The following year he became a top-class sprinter, having shown his inability to stay even a mile.

D.P. was very keen to win the Gimcrack Stakes with the Bossover colt. He would have started a hot favourite, but unfortunately started to cough a few days before the race. No woman had ever won the race, of which the owner becomes the guest of honour at the Gimcrack Dinner in December and is required by tradition to make a speech on racing politics. An all-male affair, most women would jump at the opportunity to air their views there, but most of us believed that D.P., with her antipathy to the opposite sex, would tell the noble order of Gimcracks where they could put their dinner, and that whoever made the speech of the evening it would not be the Hon. Dorothy Wyndham Paget.

This was not so. After D.P.'s death I learned that, next to the Derby, the Gimcrack was the flat race she wanted to win above all others. She was fully determined to attend the dinner, and several weeks before the race was due to be run she was composing the speech which was to set the racing community alight. It would have been a great ordeal for her to have wined and dined in the company of men, but she was determined to sacrifice herself for the pleasure of airing her views and telling the Establishment exactly what she thought of it. She was bitterly disappointed when the Bossover colt coughed his way out of the race, but she locked the speech away in a drawer, hoping that she would have the opportunity to use it on a future occasion.

I have already mentioned that D.P. took no trouble over naming her horses, and she did not find a name for the Bossover colt until he had finished his two-year-old career. D.P. eventually named him Wyndham, which was her own second name, and a far better name than Tuppence.

Although Donald Snow was still regarded as something of a playboy by the professionals, with whom he was extremely popular, his horses were admirably turned out and the Bossover colt always looked a picture. Nevertheless, to make a lifelong success as a trainer of racehorses not only must a man be dedicated, he must have a ruthless streak in his character, which the handsome Donald Snow lacked.

For a few days that summer Donald Snow took precedence over his patron as headline news. He was apt to bet beyond his means and had not D.P. come to his rescue financially it is conceivable he would have lost his licence to train.

Shortly before the outbreak of the Second World War D.P. gave up her furnished house in Balfour Place and moved to yet another furnished residence in Chalfont St Giles. Hermits Wood was an optimistic name if ever there was one. D.P. had a hundred racehorses in training, and with mares, foals, yearlings, unbroken animals in Irish pastures, show jumpers and hacks the total cannot have been far short of four hundred, although I do not think that anyone knew the exact number. She was, therefore, a public entertainer on a large scale, and as such should have been resigned to living in a blaze of publicity. On the contrary she regarded her privacy as a prize due to her by reason of her wealth, and which, if not guarded jealously, would slip away.

In point of fact the only time when she was not in the public eye was when she spent those blissful months on the banks of the Rhine with Olili and her family following Golden Miller's victory in the Grand National.

'Things will be very different now that I have moved to the country, and I shall be allowed to live in peace,' she informed her staff, though Chalfont St Giles is less than thirty miles from Piccadilly Circus. It soon became apparent that the limelight was still focused on her, but till the end of her life she failed to appreciate that by shunning publicity and snubbing those who sought to interview her she was inviting not only publicity, but a hostile Press.

On entering either Balfour Place or Hermits Wood for the first time a visitor would have gained the impression that the owner was on the point of leaving and that removal vans had already started transporting their contents to a new residence. The houses were scantily furnished, and every-where there were packages and piles of newspapers. D.P.

D

was a great hoarder. It has been said that she had execrable taste. This was not true. She had no taste at all. A chair was bought to sit on: if it did not prove comfortable she got rid of it and bought another. All articles of furniture were acquired for strictly utilitarian purposes – there was no such thing in her eyes, or so she said – as a lovely table or a handsome cabinet.

For reasons known only to herself she decided in her early twenties to eliminate all aesthetic interests from her life, which cannot have been easy for a young woman with a cultural background and who had studied music seriously enough to receive excellent notices when she had sung in public. Olili, Francis Cassel and Madame Orloff, who were her only close friends at that time, had many cultural interests, and maybe with them she showed a side of her character which she kept hidden from the rest of the world.

For the last twelve years of D.P.'s life the lovely Olili lived at Hermits Wood. Olili was fond of all animals, though not until she left her home in Germany to live in England did she take an interest in racing. She soon picked up a working knowledge of racing under both rules and after a few months could carry on an intelligent and well-informed conversation on the subject. At Hermits Wood D.P. occupied a large room on the upstairs floor while the staff carried out their duties on the ground floor, and no member of the staff ever entered her room unless she was informed that she would be 'seen'.

Sir Francis Cassel came from a racing family. Sir Ernest Cassel was a close friend of King Edward VII and was a leading owner in the early days of this century. Sir Francis accompanied D.P. to many race meetings, and worked some of her commissions for her; eventually he became an owner and, like D.P., trained with Sir Gordon Richards. Cassel was an eminent pianist, and D.P. invariably attended the annual recital he gave at the Albert Hall. In the view of Fulke Walwyn and Gordon Richards he was also a very good judge of racing, and D.P. constantly sought his opinion, though never his advice.

Gordon Richards tells the story of how he had told D.P. that one of her horses was a 'banco' (good thing) for the following day. In the case of any other owner I would have said that Gordon had told her that she could go the limit, but with D.P. there *were* no limits. Whenever she received this kind of information from her trainers she would ask all and sundry, and in particular Sir Francis, their opinion of the horse's chances. She took not the slightest notice of their answers, but for some reason she liked to have their opinions.

On this occasion Sir Francis had left for the Albert Hall when D.P. telephoned, so she sent round a note marked 'very urgent' to his dressing room, demanding his views on the prospects of this horse, running in the 2.30 race the following day. The note was delivered to Sir Francis at the interval while he was enjoying a well-earned rest, but since it demanded an immediate reply he sent a note to her box to the effect that, though he had no form books with him at the Albert Hall, he thought that the horse must have a very good chance.

D.P. derived enormous pleasure from outsmarting the opposition, which in her case comprised pretty well everyone in the racing community. In 1940, a very smart chaser she owned called Le Cygne, trained by Reggie Walker in Ireland where he had won a couple of nice races, was entered for a race at Newbury, but as she had four other horses in the race no one took much notice of Le Cygne, thought still to be in Ireland. No overnight declarations occurred in those days and owners and trainers were under no obligation to give their prospective runners to the Press, though most of them did.

Forty-eight hours before the race was due to be run D.P. had Le Cygne shipped from Ireland to Owen Anthony's stable and there was a gasp of astonishment when his number went into the frame at Newbury, neither D.P. nor her English trainer having reported that the horse had left Ireland, much less that it was going to run at Newbury. Some of the punters on the course took the 'tip' and backed Le Cygne, but with no off-the-course money for the horse D.P. obtained a much better price for her very large bet than she would have done had he appeared as a runner in the morning and mid-day papers. Le Cygne won easily and D.P. made no secret of her satisfaction at his success.

Fulke Walwyn told me the following story further illustrating D.P.'s impish sense of fun at the expense of other people. A horse she owned, trained by himself, looked a ready-made winner of a Maiden Hurdle race, but Fulke had another horse in the race, not owned by D.P., which had beaten her horse in a gallop and was likely, he thought, to prove the better in a race.

D.P. was delighted at the prospect of putting over a fast one, and agreed that Bryan Marshall should ride her horse, while the 'unknown quantity' would be ridden by a 'chalk jockey'. D.P.'s horse opened at 2–1 on, with any price offered about the stable companion. When D.P.'s agents had finished their job, however, there wasn't much to choose between them in the market. The 'springer' won as Fulke had expected him to do, and D.P. told him that the victory of this horse she did not own gave her a greater thrill than many of the races she had won with horses which carried her colours.

There can be no suggestion that there was anything in the least dishonest about these two manoeuvres, though one or two people in high places and a couple of rather prudish journalists expressed surprise that a millionairess should so mislead the public and the bookmakers. D.P.'s retort was typical of her: 'The public don't pay my training bills and the bookmakers are quite capable of looking after themselves.'

7

'Heads I win; tails it doesn't matter'

It is a common belief that deep in the heart of every despot lies a colossal inferiority complex. Hence it may be that D.P.'s refusal to co-operate as a child stemmed from a lack of self-assurance and a desire to demonstrate her independence. Under the guiding hand of Princess Mestchersky she became a normal teenager, but D.P.'s gradual realization that she was 'different' undid the Princess's good work, and her childhood fears and resentments returned, to remain with her throughout her life. She was determined to dominate others lest they dominate her and there seems little doubt that persecution mania was the reason for the barriers she erected to repel the advances of her fellow men.

Many people are born with a physical distaste for the opposite sex, but fortunately it is extremely rare for this distaste to be as acute as it was in the case of D.P. Physical contact with a man so repelled her that she would go to considerable lengths to avoid the formality of shaking hands. The only male member of her staff at Hermits Wood was the odd-job man, and he was instructed never to approach within a cricket pitch's length of his mistress.

D.P. was determined to show the world that she didn't give a damn what people thought about her. She was the only person in my experience who had no curiosity about

45

the doings of other people, all her interests being centred on herself, the occupants of Hermits Wood and her horses. Only once, to my knowledge, did she interest herself in the association of two young people: he was a jockey and the girl, the daughter of a much respected employee, a relationship she considered highly unsuitable, though I have no evidence that she was responsible for its termination.

D.P. became a byword for her eccentricity and extravagance, but in her early twenties, when she embarked on her career as an owner of racing cars and racehorses, the sporting world was well disposed towards her and considered that her likes and dislikes were her own affair. The world was less tolerant of any form of deviation in the twenties and thirties, but for the most part people minded their own business, and only the most bigoted condemned those who showed a marked preference for their own sex.

Her 'enemies', among whom she included all members of the Establishment, were a figment of her imagination, though in the years to come she was to evoke real hostility as the result of her refusal to respond to the overtures of those who wished her well. There was any amount of goodwill towards a rich young woman, whose ambition it was to win big races and who was prepared to spend unlimited money with this end in view, but D.P. eyed her well-wishers with deep suspicion and would have no truck with them.

Owen Anthony, a rotund Welshman with a beaming countenance, was an equable character and I remember him telling me soon after he became her trainer in the autumn of 1935, 'D.P. and I get on like a house on fire.' So amicable was the relationship that I am convinced he would have continued to train her jumpers for many years had he not died in the autumn of 1941. My only criticism of his training of D.P.'s horses is that he did not dissuade her from continuing to run Golden Miller at Liverpool after the horse had demonstrated that he loathed the place.

It was said of Owen that he could get away with murder, meaning that his outrageous remarks which would have given great offence if said by anyone else, invariably raised a laugh, and I never heard anyone complain that he had gone too far.

Owen was also a diplomat, with the knack of persuading D.P. that the policy he had decided on for her horses had emanated from herself. Highly strung herself she liked easy-going people, though she contributed nothing to their peace of mind by her interminable messages and telephone calls. Although she was an autocrat she disliked yes-men, and she accepted that Owen Anthony, and subsequently Fulke Walwyn and Gordon Richards, would not tolerate being messed about, called to the telephone at 2.00 a.m. or kept on race-courses until long after dark.

Owen was training the majority of D.P.'s jumpers while Walter Nightingall was training all her flat racehorses in addition to a few jumpers in 1939. One of the best horses Owen trained for her was Kilstar, who as a young horse was sold for only £60 at Tallow Fair in Ireland. Needless to say, by the time D.P. had got to hear of him his value had soared, but as he was bought privately from Captain Mark Roddick, who had won the Grand Military Gold Cup on him, his price was not divulged. Like Golden Miller, Kilstar started a short-priced favourite for the 1939 Grand National, but could only finish third, having made a mistake when going like a winner. He started favourite again the following year, but fell.

Two other top-class National Hunt horses to carry D.P.'s colours in the early days of the war were Solford and Roman Hackle, who emulated the performances of Insurance and Golden Miller in 1932 and 1933 by completing the Champion Hurdle Gold Cup double in 1940. Owen Anthony described Solford to me as the best hurdler he had ever trained, while the racing journalist Clive Graham described Roman Hackle as a 'super champion' after he had won the Gold Cup by ten lengths. These races probably needed less winning than in peacetime since with the outbreak of war a number of owners declined to run them because they thought that steeplechasing was detrimental to the war effort.

D.P. had no such qualms, but the government stepped in in 1942 and for nearly three years no jumping took place in this country. D.P., who now owned more horses than ever before transferred her jumpers to Ireland. In 1940 she had entered forty-eight horses at a two-day meeting at Cheltenham. Owen Anthony went to Ireland to train Solford, Roman Hackle, Wonersh and Kilstar, but as an old soldier who had been wounded in the First World War his heart was not in it, and he soon returned to England, where he joined the Home Guard. He died quite suddenly a few months later and his death was a sad blow to D.P. as she not only regarded him as great trainer and judge of racehorses, but she missed his jovial sense of humour. He was indeed a difficult man to replace.

D.P. was the only English owner who made no drastic reductions in her racing string during the war, and in the very limited flat racing which took place she had several horses entered in almost every race. In 1942, when rations were very scarce, she came under fierce criticism for sending twenty-two yearlings from Ireland to be trained by Walter Nightingall, and a question was asked in the House of Commons. D.P. was not unpatriotic, but rightly or wrongly she took the view that racing was essential for preserving the morale of the country, as well as the breed of horses.

By and large, the war seemed to pass her by, but – though she was at great pains to conceal it – it became known that she had financed several Women's Red Cross Units, while, unknown even to her intimate friends, she gave liberally to individual sufferers. Although her name never appeared on any list of charitable donors, I have recently discovered that throughout her life she contributed large anonymous sums. D.P. appeared to take little interest in the course of the war, but two factors troubled her greatly. Olili was at home in Germany at the outbreak of the war, and for six years she received no news of the young woman she loved above all other human beings. Her second concern was the Russian

D.P.'s father, Almeric Paget (later Lord Queenborough) when he was MP for Cambridge

Dorothy in her motor racing days, pictured with Tim Birkin

Above The Hon. Dorothy Paget on her prize-winning hunter Bloodstone

Below Dorothy Paget (facing camera) with her horse Publicity after it had won the Horley Selling Hurdle at Gatwick in 1938

Opposite above Fulke Walwyn

Opposite below The Saint, Sir Gordon Richards's first winner in his capacity as a trainer. Sir Gordon is broad side on to the camera, Miss Paget stands third from the right

Basil Briscoe

Owen Anthony

Home. She knew that its funds must be exhausted, but was powerless to act in the matter.

There is no doubt, however, that her unpopularity increased during the war, and one continually heard people ask 'What would happen if everyone behaved like D.P.?' The answer was of course that millionairesses don't grow on trees and, fortunately for the war effort, the few that were around had other interests beside racing.

D.P. paid frequent visits to Ireland to see her horses run, but it was not until I visited Ireland recently that I realized that her reputation for the straight running of her horses was not as high in that country as it was over here. Betting in the high stakes she did, a number of her beaten horses started at very short odds, but I refuse to believe that D.P. ever agreed that a horse of hers which started favourite or appeared to have an outstanding chance should be prevented from winning. I must admit, however, that there have been occasions when I wondered whether she might not have been 'put away', and I was not alone in this suspicion. D.P. was a compulsive gambler, and being immensely rich could invest huge sums without experiencing the remorse endured by most gamblers when they lose.

In other words she played a game we should all like to play, called 'Heads I win and tails it doesn't matter'. Even among the less rich the compulsive gambler experiences a greater degree of excitement from winning than he does despair from his losses. I suspect he also experiences some masochistic enjoyment while his money is in the air. D.P. loved winning, not so much by reason of profit as the satisfaction of feeling that she had outsmarted the bookmakers. When she lost, which she did heavily on balance, she never gave it another thought, and merely handed the bills to her private secretary Miss Annetta Williams, who not only made out the cheques but signed them as well.

Miss Williams was the rock which supported this strange edifice and D.P. knew that without this remarkable woman, with her vast knowledge of racing and memory like a filing cabinet, the edifice would have crumbled. Miss Clarke was her horse show secretary as well as O.C. motor-cars, and Miss Charlton, now Mrs Smirke, was her racing secretary. All three women were indispensable, and no one knew this better than D.P., though she might not have admitted it.

Miss Williams was the only secretary in my experience who not only wrote out the cheques but signed them as well. Once, when D.P. was called upon to give evidence in a case of fraud, prosecuting counsel held up a document and asked her if the signature was hers and without glancing at it she replied, 'No.' Asked by defence counsel how she knew without scrutinizing the document, she replied, 'Because I never sign cheques or documents.'

Misguided though she may have been, it was D.P.'s honest belief that her mission in life was to keep racing going during the Second World War. In addition to providing sport for the millions, flat racing is the key to the bloodstock industry, and unless the sires and dams of tomorrow are tested on the racecourse the breeders have no means of establishing which horses are best fitted to hand on their blood to posterity. It was essential, therefore, that the classics and other top-class races should take place, while every precaution should be taken that those functions did not hinder the war effort.

Jumping, however, is a very different matter, and it is hard to justify meetings being held in wartime at which ninety per cent of the runners are geldings or elderly mares, who would be most unlikely to produce a classic winner. However, D.P. maintained that racing under both rules was indispensable if the morale of the country was to remain at a high level, though I find it hard to believe that soldiers, sailors or airmen were greatly inspired by the knowledge that racing was taking place at Plumpton. Her ingenious argument that the running of geldings was of great assistance to breeders in that it revealed which sires and dams were producing winners was not wholly convincing, and cut no ice with the government.

Having had five times as many runners as any other owner

D.P. headed the list of winning owners in the 1940–1 season.
For once in a way, however, the big Cheltenham meeting
proved disastrous. She and Owen Anthony were confident
that Solford and Roman Hackle would repeat their victories
of the previous year in the Champion Hurdle and Gold Cup,
but neither horse could finish in the first three. D.P. valued
Roman Hackle at £10,000, though no one would have paid
a fifth of that price for a jumper in wartime, and it was ironic
that this wartime Gold Cup was won by Poet Prince, who
had cost his owner, Mr Sherbrooke, only forty guineas.

Some idea of the amount of money it must have cost D.P.
to keep a large stable of jumpers in training in wartime may
be gleaned from the fact that as leading owner she won
fourteen races of a total value of only £1,325. She won no
race of importance in Ireland but her Golden Jack proved
himself the best novice chaser there, winning nine races, and
the following year ran the mighty Prince Regent to a length
in the Irish Grand National.

Although she won three races in one day at the opening
of the flat racing season at Lincoln, none of her four entries
for the Lincoln Handicap could run, and the race was won
by the Hon. George Lambton's Gloaming, ridden by a small
seventeen-year-old apprentice, David Dick. Eleven years later
Dave won the Gold Cup at Cheltenham in D.P.'s colours on
Mont Tremblant, trained by Fulke Walwyn.

D.P. had bought Bakhtawar, a half-brother to the Triple
Crown winner Bahram, from the Aga Khan, but once again
a close relative of a great horse was to prove himself a wash-
out, and like the notorious Colonel Payne he was trained by
Fred Darling. But he could not be trained as a two-year-old;
while having shown promise in a gallop at Beckhampton, he
fell lame and had to be scratched from the Derby. He was
still a maiden when he ran in the St Leger, in which he finished
fifth.

Tommy Carey had ridden for D.P. with great success under
Pony Turf Club Rules at Northolt just before the war, and
now he was retained by her to ride her horses trained at

Epsom by Walter Nightingall. D.P. sent a message to Fred Darling, by her secretary, that she wanted Carey to ride one of her horses trained by him. Gordon Richards was first jockey for Beckhampton, and Fred replied most courteously that he would be very grateful if Miss Paget would remove her horses from his stable that afternoon. Needless to say, Gordon rode the horse in question.

Following the death of Owen Anthony, Solford was trained at Epsom by Bill Payne as a chaser, but at Worcester, on only his second appearance in a steeplechase he fell at the water jump and broke his back. Solford had been a great favourite of D.P., and in addition to his numerous successes over hurdles had won an Irish Cambridgeshire; she was thus very upset at the loss of this good horse, and it was only a very small consolation to her on this tragic afternon when Duna and Easy Chair, both heavily backed, completed a double for her.

The Scout of the *Daily Express* wrote in January 1942 that Miss Dorothy Paget would be entering dozens of horses at practically every meeting that season, and went on to record that the victory of a horse called Verbatim had broken a losing sequence of forty. Even then, D.P. had to wait while her horse survived an objection before she collected the £100 prize. Although the 1941–2 jumping season was much curtailed, the incredible fact is that D.P., with more horses than any other six owners put together did not win a single steeplechase.

After three years of war most yearlings fetched a quarter of what they would have done in peacetime, but at the Newmarket October sales of 1942 D.P. paid the top price of 4,800 guineas for a colt by Blue Peter out of Centeno, and sent him to be trained by Fred Darling.

No member of her staff could remember how often D.P. had consoled herself, after some extremely expensive horse had proved himself useless, with the words, 'Never mind, I'll win the Derby before I die.' And win it she did in 1943, though the race was a substitute event, run over the July course at Newmarket, and worth only £4,388 to the winner.

D.P. had sent the majority of her flat racehorses and a few jumpers to be trained by Walter Nightingall at Epsom towards the end of 1935, and her first winner trained by him was Wheatley, ridden by Joe Marshall, who had won the 1929 Derby on Trigo. Walter and sister Marjorie, who acted as his assistant trainer, were a hundred per cent professional, though Walter was a somewhat nervy individual, lacking in patience, and had not the ideal temperament for the job of training for England's most exacting owner. However, the partnership lasted for twelve years and Walter trained her Straight Deal to win the 1943 Derby, D.P.'s only classic success in thirty years during which she spent hundreds of thousands of pounds in an endeavour to buy and subsequently breed the best horses in the world.

8

Wartime austerity and the break with Nightingall

1943 was a great year for D.P., Nightingall and Carey. On the same afternoon that Straight Deal won the Derby, they won the Coventry Stakes with Orestes (Donatello-Orison). Orestes subsequently proved himself the best two-year-old of his year by winning the Middle Park Stakes, and also the best two-year-old she had ever owned. At the end of that season she was leading owner, sixteen of her horses having won twenty-six races, value £13,146.

Straight Deal, a medium-sized bay colt, won over six furlongs at Salisbury and Windsor as a two-year-old, but though he finished second to Umiddad in the Dewhurst Stakes, Walter Nightingall regarded him as no more than a useful, honest colt who would pay his way as a three-year-old. This view was supported by the fact that though he was by Solario (jointly with Hyperion, the most expensive stallion then at stud) his dam, Good Deal, came from an undistinguished family, though she had proved herself a good race mare, winning seven races worth £4,000.

Straight Deal wintered exceptionally well, and Marjorie Nightingall relates that although good as gold on a racecourse, he was a bit of a handful on Epsom Downs in the mornings when he got loose on several occasions. Yet he appeared well able to take care of himself for, although on one occasion it was over an hour before they were able to catch him, he never came to any harm. Straight Deal could only finish sixth in the Two Thousand Guineas, but he had a confused reaction when the leaders dropped out suddenly leaving him with the whole of Newmarket Heath in front of him. Carey was therefore determined to keep him covered up as long as possible in the Derby.

Between the Guineas and Derby, Straight Deal came on dramatically. In his final gallop before he was sent to Newmarket Walter asked him a pretty big question and Straight Deal came up with the right answer. After breakfast that morning Walter telephoned D.P., who, as was her custom, was just going to bed, and told her he would be very disappointed if Straight Deal did not win the Derby.

D.P., therefore, had a series of good bets on her Derby colt; but the market on the Derby is very strong, even in wartime, and on the day of the race he was a 100–6 chance. D.P.'s luck on the flat had been so atrocious that backers had despaired of her ever winning a big race; in any case, Straight Deal was taking on the Aga Khan's two colts Nasrullah and Umiddad, and the latter had beaten him comfortably as a two-year-old.

It was almost impossible to make an accurate assessment of the merits of a classic field in wartime, as very few of the horses remained in training after the end of their three-year-old careers, and therefore only met horses of their own generation. I consider, however, that the 1943 Derby field was well up to standard. The race was a real thriller. Persian Gulf led for one and a quarter miles, when he was headed by Nasrullah (Gordon Richards) and Umiddad (Charlie Elliott.) Until close to home it appeared certain that the Aga Khan's colts would finish first and second, but in the final hundred yards Carey brought Straight Deal up with a perfectly timed run to take the lead in the last few strides and beat Umiddad by a head with Nasrullah half a length away, third.

Wearing the famous tweed overcoat she called 'speckled hen', D.P. led in her winner, and was given a great ovation. She was not the most popular of owners at that time, but racegoers love a trier and D.P.'s never-say-die attitude in the face of ill fortune, which would have daunted ninety-nine owners out of a hundred, had warmed them to her. It was a good moment, and as the gallant Straight Deal was led out of the winning enclosure a beaming D.P. commanded Walter and Marjorie Nightingall and Bob Lyall to meet her after the last race, adding, 'We'll go along and see Straight Deal in his stable (he was not being sent back to Epsom till the following day), and have a little celebration.'

Bob Lyall was the racing correspondent of *The Times*, and was the only pressman D.P. would allow within fifty yards of her. In addition to being a first-class journalist, Bob was an amusing companion, so D.P. may have liked him – so long, of course, as he did not come too close. Though she really had no choice; at that time Bob was seldom more than a length of a horse away from Marjorie Nightingall's side, so if you had horses in training with her brother, you had to accept Bob. No man enjoyed a party more than Bob Lyall, especially in wartime when such luxuries were few and far between, and he was rubbing his hands in anticipation as he told his colleagues in the Press room that D.P. was going to push the boat out that evening, and that he'd been invited. Dreams of the popping of champagne corks, however, were dispelled when, having given Straight Deal a congratulatory pat, D.P. extracted her brandy flask from her copious 'blue and yellow' racing handbag and, having taken a swig at it herself, handed it round. That was the 'celebration'!

But if the festivities were small, the cause was a good one. Carey had ridden a most artistic race on Straight Deal demonstrating that this forgotten man, who had only received a licence to ride under Jockey Club Rules two years earlier, could stand comparison with Gordon Richards, Charlie Elliott,

Charlie Smirke and the other leading riders of his day. After his apprenticeship with Stanley Wootton, Carey had disappeared from the racing scene through lack of patronage, emerging several years later as a leading rider under Pony Turf Club Rules at Northolt. D.P., ever on the look-out for a new toy, decided to patronize pony racing with Pat Donoghue, son of the immortal Steve, as her trainer. Every owner with a large string has a number of undersized animals, and D.P. was no exception; at Northolt these ponies were very successful. Tommy Carey became her jockey and won any number of races for her, including the Northolt Derby on Scottish Rifle. Racing at Northolt folded up with the outbreak of war, and D.P. applied to the Jockey Club for a licence for Carey to ride her horses trained by Nightingall. This was granted and, with Nightingall as her trainer and Carey as her jockey, D.P. enjoyed greater success than at any time in her career as an owner of flat racehorses.

As for the Derby winner himself, Straight Deal subsequently won a 1½-mile race at Ascot in great style and started favourite for the St Leger, but could only finish third to two exceptionally good fillies, Lord Derby's Herringbone and Lord Rosebery's Ribbon.

Racing was, of course, very much restricted during the war, and it was only to be expected that such a self-indulgent lady as D.P. would take unkindly to the general austerities of the time. It was not an attitude calculated to win her many friends. One of her favourite announcements was that the war was being fought simply for the purpose of inflicting the maximum inconvenience on her, and another that 'easily the worst thing about the war is that I sometimes have to travel by train'. In peacetime she had almost invariably travelled by car and, on the rare occasion when she patronized the railways, had reserved a carriage for herself. In wartime, when every train was packed to capacity, private individuals were quite rightly prohibited from reserving compartments. So when she travelled by train she might have to suffer the indignity of sitting next to a man, possibly one she had never

57

E

seen before. She therefore wrote a letter to the Minister of Transport requesting that the ban on the reservation of railway carriages should be lifted in her case, explaining that the proximity of a strange male person invariably made her vomit. The Minister replied that although he regretted any inconvenience that the Hon. Dorothy Paget might undergo as a result of measures he might be forced to adopt in the interests of the war effort, he was unable to accede to her request.

Just before the outbreak of war, on the way home from Liverpool by train, she had reserved a table for herself and ordered four steaks. When these were cooked the waiter asked her if she would like to start right away or wait for her guests. 'Guests?' she answered. 'Who said anything about guests?' She had long lost her figure, and this was particularly noticeable because she wore no sort of support. Her appetite, always large, had not at that time assumed the proportions it did in her later years, and it is possible that the four steaks were ordered so that she could keep the table for herself. History does not relate whether she ate all four between Liverpool and Euston.

D.P. was basically abstemious, and her only alcoholic drink, apart from her brandy flask, was a minute portion of champagne in a tumbler of orange juice. On the other hand she was a very heavy smoker, and would get through anything up to a hundred cigarettes in the course of twenty-four hours. She always smoked through a holder, and, except when they became unobtainable during the war, nothing but Balkan Sobranies (Turkish).

For her numerous cars, she obtained a petrol ration and when there was no further issue for private individuals, she fell back on hired vehicles. 'If you're caught I'll pay the fine,' she would tell the driver, to which one replied, 'What happens if I get sent to prison – will you go instead?' She thought this very funny, but she thought it less funny when she was caught out on a visit to Salisbury Races.

In the *Daily Express* of 15 July 1943 the following item appeared:

The Hon. Dorothy Paget, race horse owner and winner of the 1943 Derby, of Hermits Wood, Chalfont St Giles, Bucks, was summoned at Marlborough Street for using motor fuel in a hired vehicle for a journey to Salisbury race course on 17 April and doing a journey outside the 'inner radius' without having signed and delivered the necessary declaration to the proprietor of the vehicle. Mr L. Byrne, for Miss Paget, said she pleaded guilty, but unfortunately could not be present as she was indisposed.

The Marlborough Street Magistrate, Mr J. B. Sambach, K.C., declined to deal with the case in the absence of Miss Paget and hoped that she would be well enough to attend the Court in the course of a few days. Nine days later a further item appeared to the effect that Miss Paget had attended Marlborough Street Police Court and had been fined £25 with ten guineas costs. I was told by a reporter who was present that Mr Sambach strongly advised Miss Paget not to appear before him again on a similar charge.

Soon after the war D.P. was on her way to a race meeting when her car broken down. The only vehicle in sight was a butcher's delivery van. 'Hop out and buy it,' she told her secretary, who was sitting beside her. The butcher demanded £300, which was promptly paid, and D.P. is alleged to have arrived at the meeting sitting between two carcasses. From that day onwards, she suffered from a phobia about her car breaking down, and she never set off, even on the shortest journey, without a second car following in her wake. If she was going any distance, a third car followed the second, in case that also broke down. Occasionally as many as four cars were employed in convoy, with a secretary sent on ahead in yet another car to ensure that everything would be in order on her arrival. D.P. had not learned the art of motor-racing from Tim Birkin for nothing, and she drove very fast with a high degree of skill. In charge of her motorcars (she never had less than six at a time) was Miss Clarke, a highly-skilled mechanic and a first-class driver. The only qualification demanded of her numerous secretaries was that they could drive a car. All of them could type, though some of them with only one finger. As they were almost exclusively employed in answering the telephone, making seven copies of every message received, and in relaying them to D.P. and all the other members of her staff, this was of no great consequence. They were also sent on numerous errands and were required to check out and check in on their return.

D.P. spent a large part of her day – or perhaps I should say night, as she rose at approximately 8.00 p.m. and went to bed at 8.00 a.m. – in making work for her secretaries. Some of her junior members could not stand the strain for more than a few months, and there was a constant stream of secretaries coming and going.

To return to 1943, D.P.'s great year, it was, after her long series of failures, a great triumph for her to become only the second owner to win both the Grand National and Derby. Her predecessor was King Edward VII; as Prince of Wales, he won both races in 1900 with Ambush and Diamond Jubilee, who went on to win the Triple Crown. It was in the course of this year that Walter Nightingall found he could not accommodate all the horses D.P. wished to send him, so the surplus were sent to be trained by Captain Ossie Bell at Lambourn. Walter was indeed a fortunate man, for whereas most trainers had been crying out for horses during the war, he never had a single empty box.

D.P. was naturally overjoyed at the victories of Straight Deal, Orestes and other useful horses trained by Nightingall, but her partnership with him was never entirely harmonious. D.P. was proving very difficult, and Walter did not possess the sunny disposition of Owen Anthony, who would tell her with a beaming smile that he would not stand for an owner who arranged to inspect her horses at 7 p.m. and then arrived several hours later. Walter fussed and fumed and was not pacified even when D.P. doled out fivers to employees who had been standing at their charges' heads for three hours.

It was not, however, until December 1947, more than four years after Straight Deal's Derby victory, that the breach occurred. Although she was in constant touch with her trainer

D.P. insisted that he write her a detailed report every week on every one of the thirty horses he trained for her. Like every other trainer at that time he was short of labour, and with entries, forfeits, and the business of running a short-handed stable of around fifty horses (he was was not her private trainer), the extra work, which he considered entirely unnecessary, nearly drove him mad.

Although there were no big winners among them, Walter Nightingall won twenty-seven races for D.P. in 1945 – twenty-two on the flat and five over the jumps. Every owner prefers to win an important race, but prize money was of secondary importance to D.P.: if she could win a five-figure bet on some humble event she was happy enough. Her most important success in 1946 was with Distel in the Champion Hurdle, but he was trained in Ireland. D.P. brought off a hat-trick on that memorable day at Cheltenham, her other winners being Dunshaughlin in the N.H. Handicap Chase and Loyal King in the Grand Annual Handicap Chase. All three were trained in Ireland.

D.P. had high hopes of bringing off the Champion Hurdle–Gold Cup double at Cheltenham for the third time, with Distel and Happy Home. But the meeting was postponed and when the races were eventually held D.P.'s horses disappointed her. Their failure was not surprising as the races were won respectively by National Spirit and Fortina, two horses in the class of Insurance and Golden Miller.

Ten years had passed since D.P. had paid 15,000 guineas for Colonel Payne, and backers who had subsequently lost a fortune over him had been doing their best to forget him: he had won three races of a total value of £344. He had not been seen around for a long time when he was led into the Sale Ring and knocked down to Captain K. Freeman for 250 guineas and there was a sigh of relief when his new owner, who was in battledress, said he intended not to race him but to stand him as a stallion or sell him to go abroad. D.P. was always reluctant to sell her horses, and having listed seventeen for sale at Newmarket she withdrew nine of them without giving any reason. Such changes of heart were typical of her and infuriated auctioneers and would-be purchasers throughout her career.

In 1946 D.P. decided to send some of her horses to be trained by Fulke Walwyn, and Jean, Lady Ashcombe told me the following story of how Fulke came to hear that he was to become D.P.'s trainer. Lady Ashcombe and her young son were staying in a hotel in Cheltenham, and her son complained at breakfast that he had not slept a wink as Miss Paget, who had the next room, had talked on the telephone throughout the night. 'Did you hear anything of interest?' his mother asked him. 'Not much,' he replied, 'excepting that she's going to train with Fulke' (the Walwyns were great friends). At the races he approached Fulke and said, 'Congratulations on becoming Dorothy Paget's trainer.' 'I know nothing about it,' Fulke replied. 'That's as may be,' the boy said, 'but you are.' And he was.

At about the same time, D.P. engaged another trainer, and sent a dozen of her flat racehorses to be trained by Jelliss at Newmarket. At the end of 1946 Tommy Carey retired from the saddle because of increasing weight, the only flat race jockey D.P. ever retained and with whom in the years he rode for her she enjoyed the most success. Looking back on those years, it is hard to believe that had it not been for the introduction of pony racing and D.P.'s decision to run some of her smaller horses under P.T.C. rules, Carey would have remained in obscurity.

In January 1947 the following notice appeared in the Racing Calendar:

The Windsor stewards enquired into the running of Broad Atlantic in the Keats Long Distance Hurdle Race, which he won by eight lengths at 11–10 compared with his running in his two previous races. Having heard the evidence of Miss Paget, Miss Nightingall, representing the trainer who was abroad, and T. Issac, jockey, they were not satisfied with the explanations given, and referred the matter to the stewards of the N. H. Committee.

The following week a further notice appeared in the Racing Calendar:

The stewards of the N.H. Committee met at Cheltenham to enquire into the running of Miss Dorothy Paget's horse Broad Atlantic at Windsor compared with its previous running, and accepted the explanation of the owner and jockey.

The enquiry had lasted one and a half hours. At the end of it, needless to say, D.P. had no comment to make to the Press, but Tommy Issac said, 'Everything is OK, but the stewards had one or two things to say to me.'

The long and successful partnership between D.P. and Walter Nightingall ended that year, though I do not know whether the enquiry into the running of Broad Atlantic had anything to do with it. The final row – and they had become more frequent with the passing years – took place at Sandown, and the voices of the two parties echoed round the paddock.

For only the second time in her life D.P. issued a statement to the Press requesting that the following telegram to her trainer should be published:

A mutual apology for the most inglorious and undignified behaviour on both sides might have been possible, but you have made this impossible through making this private matter public property, so am sending for my ten remaining horses as soon as possible. Regret that having won the Derby together we had to part in such an unnecessary flamboyant stupid manner, but nevertheless I on my part bear no malice and hope you win another Derby for someone else soon. Many thanks for the pleasure we used to enjoy in years gone by.

Wheatley, in a hurdle race at Gatwick on 28 February 1936, was the first winner saddled by Nightingall for D.P., and Master Builder, in a flat race on 15 November 1947, was the last. In all, he trained 210 winners for D.P., 163 on the flat and forty-seven over jumps.

9

More trainers, winners and near misses

By the end of the war D.P. was breeding sufficient horses to keep all her trainers in England and Ireland fully occupied, but that did not prevent her going to market when some fashionably-bred youngster came up for sale. Despite all the reverses she had suffered with yearlings bought at public auction, she still believed she could buy as well as breed a classic winner.

Her most expensive brood mare was the six-year-old Sister Clara, who had changed hands as a yearling for only twenty guineas but for whom she paid 11,000 guineas. D.P. had previously paid 6,600 guineas for Sister Clara's yearling daughter by Stardust. Orestes on the other hand, who had failed to realize expectations as a three-year-old, she sold for a mere 5,100 guineas, a fifth of the price he would have fetched at the end of his two-year-old career.

Some years earlier D.P. had paid 4,000 guineas for Sister Clara's half brother Clarendon. Trained by Fred Darling Clarendon never won a race, though at one time it was thought he might be a Derby colt but having been gelded, Clarendon was eventually sold by D.P. for 140 guineas. Some idea of the scale on which she was now racing may be gleaned from the fact that she had forty horses entered for the 1944 classics, while the Aga Khan had only twenty-five.

At the outbreak of the war the Aga Khan either sold or leased about eighty per cent of his horses. After the war his son Aly Khan told me, 'Father hoped he'd be proved wrong, but he was certain Hitler would win and was determined not to be caught with his trousers down.' After El Alamein and Stalingrad the Aga Khan began buying again, and at the Newmarket sales of 1944 his representative actually outbid D.P., when he gave £13,125 for a son of Hyperion and £11,550 for a son of Blue Peter. D.P. was the underbidder on both occasions, a unique experience for her. Could she at last be learning a little sense?

In the course of the war D.P. engaged yet another trainer, Captain Ossie Bell, who had trained with great success for many years for Lord Londonderry and Sir Hugo Cunliffe-Owen. The best horse trained by Bell for D.P. was Mrs Feather, who won numerous good races and finished third in the One Thousand Guineas to Lord Derby's Sun Stream and Lord Rosebery's Blue Smoke.

When jumping was resumed on an extensive scale in this country in 1945, D.P. won three races in one afternoon at the Cheltenham Christmas meeting with Hamlet, Astrometer and Housewarmer, all trained in Ireland and ridden by Dan Moore, and was delighted at her hat-trick, especially as in Happy Home she owned a chaser she knew to be vastly superior to this trio. As jumping had not been interrupted in Ireland, Irish-trained jumpers were at a big advantage over their English rivals. D.P. was winning jumping races galore in Ireland, and actually brought off six doubles at six consecutive meetings.

When the war was over D.P. could not find immediate accommodation in England for her Irish-trained horses so continued to have them trained there and sent over to England for their engagements. Before the days of air travel for horses this constituted quite a problem.

At the end of 1945 Housewarmer had won three steeplechases and four of her Irish-trained jumpers had won eight races between them. Clive Graham wrote in the *Daily Express*

that D.P. had an unrivalled stableful of chasers and hurdlers
in Ireland under the shrewd supervision of Charlie 'Romeo'
Rogers. Charlie Rogers was a man of great charm and early
in their association D.P. had nicknamed him 'Romeo', which
was universally adopted by his acquaintances.

Dan Moore was now D.P.'s regular jockey. He had been a
leading rider in Ireland for a number of years and D.P. was
only one of many in England who considered him without a
superior at that time. But D.P.'s Distel, who was proving
himself a great hurdler, was always ridden by M. Gordon.
Although the horse had proved himself a top-class flat race
performer, he would consent to go for no other jockey.

D.P. had high hopes that her Sun Storm would prove himself another Straight Deal, and after he had beaten Lord
Astor's Court Martial at Salisbury she backed him to win the
Two Thousand Guineas and Derby. But for no apparent
reason Sun Storm took a violent dislike to racing, running
atrociously in both races, and subsequently at Ascot kicked a
filly call Sun Strap so bady that she could not run again for
weeks.

Long before her final break with Walter Nightingall, D.P.
had been negotiating with the Newmarket trainer Henri
Jelliss and his son Harry to train her horses, and already a
number of them had left Epsom for Newmarket. The partnership was doomed to failure from the start. Seldom can there
have been a more ill-assorted combination of business
associates. Henri Jelliss a hardworking professional, revelled
in tradition and having been a jockey of the old school, was
now a trainer in that style. Owners were in a class of their
own, and at their approach you touched your cap, while in
certain circumstances you actually removed it. Trainers were
invariably addressed as 'Mr' by jockeys, while both trainers
and jockeys never carried on a conversation with an owner
without a liberal sprinkling of Sirs or Madams.

With her utter contempt for convention, D.P. was like no
other owner Jelliss had ever encountered. Although not far
short of fifty, she was still unmarried so he could not call her

Madam. At the same time she neither looked nor behaved like a Miss. Her retinue of secretaries left him completely bewildered, and Francis Cassel was not at all his cup of tea. A number of owners Henri Jelliss had ridden for, whilst not exactly out of the top drawer, had conformed to the pattern expected of an owner. But D.P., the daughter of a Lord, behaved in a way he found mystifying and slightly shocking.

Neither Henri Jelliss nor his son Harry, between whom the horses alternated every few months, were prigs or prudes. It was simply that they could not understand the Hon. Dorothy Wyndham Paget. They had never met anyone remotely like her, and they made no secret of the fact that they hoped they never would again. Although their telephone rang continually with calls from Hermits Wood, there was no proper communication between this highly unconventional owner and her two conventional trainers and it was therefore surprising that the association lasted as long as it did.

A horse called Birthday Greetings was one of the reasons. A brilliant two-year-old he won the Richmond Stakes at Goodwood most impressively from a big black colt by Rhodes Scholar called Black Tarquin. The two colts were due to meet again in the Gimcrack Stakes, in which Black Tarquin received a pull of 7 lb. Birthday Greetings had appeared to beat Black Tarquin with all that in hand at Goodwood, but whereas Birthday Greetings was already mature, Black Tarquin appeared more backward, though he was already a winner. The question was whether or not Black Tarquin could have made up the leeway.

Captain Boyd Rochfort and his jockey Harry Carr thought he had, but D.P. realizing that for only the third time in her career she owned a top-class two-year-old, unearthed that old Gimcrack speech and brought it up to date. Needless to say, she also backed Birthday Greetings to win her a large sum, and he started at even money.

After a great race Black Tarquin was adjudged the winner by a neck from Birthday Greetings, but the latter's jockey, Eph Smith, promptly lodged an objection for boring. The

67

Press stand at York in those days was only a few feet from ground level and well past the winning post, so I had no idea of the right or wrongs of the case. The stewards had no mechanical aids, and were unable to arrive at an agreement. Consequently over fifty minutes elapsed before they gave the benefit of the doubt to the actual winner Black Tarquin. This long wait was agony for D.P. and when the white flag was hoisted, denoting that the objection had been overruled, she put away her speech, and, with a heavy heart, boarded her plane for home.

Never again was she to own a horse who appeared likely to enable her to speak her mind to the racing community.

Although D.P. and Henri Jelliss did not shout at one another in the paddock the final bust-up was just as undignified and attracted as much publicity as when D.P. and Walter Nightingall had parted company. The *Daily Express* carried the following item on 18 July 1950:

Henri Jelliss, who has trained racehorses for Miss Dorothy Paget at Newmarket for six years has written asking her to remove them from his stables. He said last night, 'Miss Paget has not so far replied. I have about twelve of her horses including Good Record (twice a winner), Angelico (three wins), and Miss Mop (one win). I also trained Silver Gate for the flat. It won ten races. Miss Paget ran it over the jumps, and instead of returning it to me transferred it to one of her other trainers, Mr Johnson-Houghton at Blewbury.

'So far as I know Miss Paget had always been perfectly satisfied with the way I trained her horses.

'During the whole of the time I have been training for her she has visited my stables once. That was three years ago. We have met only once this year, at a race meeting two months ago. I would have instructions to box a horse for a race meeting the following day and then get a telegram on the morning of the race saying that the horse was being scratched. I have found it difficult to carry on under these conditions.'

At her home Hermits Wood, Chalfont St Giles, Bucks, Miss Paget issued this statement early today saying, 'Mr Jelliss's statement is inaccurate over many points. I have not been perfectly satisfied as Mr Jellis said, but I hoped he would carry on and we would part quietly at the end of the season. The final break was not over Silver Gate which had been gone into several months ago. My horse Miss Mop was the cause of the break.'

So incensed was Jelliss that he sent her a telephone message that if the remaining horses belonging to her were not removed from his yard in the course of the next twelve hours he would open their boxes and turn them loose.

D.P. adopted the same pattern of procedure when she left Jelliss as when she had left Walter Nightingall. Now Gordon Johnson-Houghton was the lucky man. Her practice was to send two or three horses to her new trainer on the pretext that a change would do the animals good, and then when twenty or thirty yearlings from her studs at Ballymacoll and Elsenham came into training they would follow them to him. The old trainer would be left with half a dozen or so deadbeats, and in consequence he would invariably ask her to remove them.

She adopted this devious method, not because she feared a confrontation – moral cowardice was certainly not one of her shortcomings – but in order to try out the new man. In the same way that those who make a habit of marriage invariably believe that the new one is going to make up for all previous disappointments, D.P. always believed that the new trainer possessed all the virtues of his predecessors but, more important still, none of their shortcomings. There was, therefore, no real necessity for D.P. to give her new trainer a trial run, as for the first few months at any rate he could do no wrong in her eyes.

I have only met about half a dozen trainers in my fifty years on the Turf who did not carry a chip on their shoulders the size of a telegraph pole, and if all owners had been as fickle as D.P. their number would have been even less, though Fulke Walwyn, to name just one, emerged unscathed from the ordeal.

Alec Law, Basil Briscoe, Owen Anthony, Donald Snow, Bill Payne, Walter Nightingall, Henri Jelliss, Harry Jelliss,

Fulke Walwyn, Gordon Johnson-Houghton, Frank Butters, Fred Darling, Ossie Bell, Marcus Marsh, Charles Jerdein, Sir Gordon Richards and 'Frenchy' Nicholson all trained for D.P. in this country, and if I have missed anyone out I offer him my humble apology.

As she owned the largest string of horses in the country, expected every horse to be treated as a VIP and insisted on written reports every week, it may seem surprising that D.P. did not appoint a private trainer. The reason, I think, was that she realized that no man would remain in her employment indefinitely, and she did not relish the idea of having to continue to pay his salary until his contract expired. With a public trainer her obligation ceased on the day her horses left his yard.

Although D.P. did not win any outstanding races in 1948 she enjoyed a wonderfully successful season. Established as a leading breeder, the large sums of money she paid for brood mares were now paying far bigger dividends than had her profligate spending on fashionably-bred colts and fillies at the yearling sales. In 1948 she bred the winners of sixty-two races with thirty-one horses, and her winnings totalled £34,000. One racing correspondent wrote 'Never before in British Turf history have so many races been won in a single season by horses all bred by the same person.'

The Ballymacoll stud in Co. Meath had not yet got under way, and these winners were all bred at the Elsenham stud in Essex, which D.P. had bought from my uncle, Sir Walter Gilbey, in 1936. Straight Deal, who had been there, was now standing at this stud, and in 1948 ten of his progeny won twenty-one races worth £9,441. In 1953 he took up stud duties at Ballymacoll.

On one afternoon under N.H. Rules at Folkestone D.P. won the first five races with animals trained by Fulke Walwyn and ridden by Bryan Marshall. She is alleged to have said that she was disappointed, as she had expected all six, but she was afraid that the one which got beaten, Loyal Monarch (he finished second), was not too genuine. The five winners were

Langis Son, Loyal King, Endless, Jack Tatters and Legal Joy.

D.P. thought nothing of entering a horse in a selling race of £100, winner to be sold for £100, and then buying it in for a four-figure sum after it had won. In those days the surplus over and above the selling price was divided between the owner of the second horse and the racecourse executive; she was therefore a godsend to these two deserving causes. Realizing she was determined to retain her winner at all costs, the owner of the second horse invariably ran her up.

On one occasion at Leicester, having won races with Jack Tatters and Tredivion, her horse Coventry was disqualified after winning a selling hurdle race. Anyone could claim a horse other than a winner, and if two or more persons claimed the same horse an auction was held between the claimants. Any surplus above the claiming price and the value of the race was divided between the Race Fund and the Bentinck Benevolent Fund. There were several claims for Coventry when it was known that the objection had been sustained, and he fetched 1,000 guineas at the auction, leaving £600 to be divided between the two funds. The successful claimant passed Coventry back to D.P., presumably at a profit, so it can be assumed that it cost D.P. upwards of £1,000 to retain a winner who had been disqualified, plus her losing bet. This, I have little doubt, ran well into four figures. Running horses in selling races when plans went astray could be a very expensive business for D.P.

Her best flat racehorses at this time were Birthday Greetings, Star Witness and Fine Prospect. After his somewhat unlucky defeat in the Gimcrack Stakes, Birthday Greetings, trained by Jelliss, was beaten by a whisker in the Middle Park Stakes by The Cobbler. He was well fancied for the Two Thousand Guineas, but could only finish fourth to My Babu, The Cobbler and Pride of India.

Distel, winner of the 1946 Champion Hurdler, and in his day virtually on a par with Insurance, had seemingly turned a rogue, for on one occasion he refused the start and on another occasion the fourth hurdle; he was put down in

71

January 1948 when found to be suffering from chronic heart disease for which there is no cure. Horses are often much maligned, and when a top-class performer appears to have lost his zest for racing, in nine cases out of ten there is a valid reason for his reluctance.

With Happy Home D.P. came very close to winning her seventh Gold Cup, but he was beaten one and a half lengths by Cottage Rake, who won the race three years running. This titanic struggle between two superlative jumpers, each as brave as a lion, brought back memories of that epic race between Golden Miller and Thomond II thirteen years earlier. The favourite, Cool Customer, fell at the first fence, and after Klaxton, who had set a great gallop, had faded, Cottage Rake looked to have the race well won when Martin Molony, riding like a man inspired, forced Happy Home level with him again and they jumped the last fence in the same stride. On the flat, however, Cottage Rake, who had won the Irish Cesarewitch, drew away inch by inch to win an unforgettable race. Happy Home was probably the third best chaser (Golden Miller and Mont Tremblant were the first two), owned by D.P., and he was unlucky to run up against two superb horses in Fortina and Cottage Rake in successive years.

10

Success with Fulke Walwyn

D.P. seldom named a horse until she was forced to do so – which was before it ran as a three-year-old – but on one occasion she was able to postpone a christening till the horse in question was four because it was always lame and could not run in its first two seasons. She eventually called it Tennyson, and as it was by Straight Deal out of Fille de Poète it wasn't a bad name. Fille de Poète was the dam of The Phoenix, winner of the Irish Derby, so Tennyson was beautifully bred and sound enough to run at Leicester in his four-year-old career (the *Daily Express* pointed out that few owners could afford to keep a horse in training at £6 a week for three years before running him). Tennyson did not appear to be greatly fancied but, ridden by Charlie Smirke, he upset odds of 5–2 laid on Land Baby, ridden by Gordon Richards. He won three more races that season and finished second in the 1949 Eclipse Stakes to M. Boussac's Djeddah, so D.P.'s patience was rewarded. Few horses which do not run till they are four years old come so near to winning one of our greatest races.

By this time D.P. had parted company with the Jelliss family, Tennyson and the majority of her flat racehorses being trained by Johnson-Houghton whose brother-in-law, Fulke Walwyn, now trained all D.P.'s jumpers and also a few of her horses on the flat – including Aldborough, by Straight Deal out of Pilch by Windsor Lad. Aldborough was undoubtedly the best out-and-out stayer to carry the blue and yellow jacket, and Gordon Richards believed that that he would have carried top weight 9.3 successfully in the Cesarewitch had he not collided with one of the posts which substituted for rails on the Rowley Mile course at Newmarket.

Aldborough had previously run in the Doncaster Cup and, though he was no match for Alycidon, one of the greatest stayers of all time, he would have won that race by six lengths had not Lord Derby's horse been in the field. Early that season he won the Guildford Handicap at Sandown by five lengths with 9.8 in the saddle, and from then onwards he was set to carry mammoth weights.

Aldborough had no Alycidon to meet in the following year's Doncaster Cup and, beautifully ridden by Doug Smith, he won by two lengths from High Forest with the French horse Vic Day three lengths away third. D.P. was unwell, and unable to see Aldborough win her the most important long-distance flat race of her career. Judging from the performances of some of the horses which finished behind him, Aldborough might have won the Gold Cup at Ascot had he run in that race. Although he was by D.P.'s Derby winner Straight Deal, Aldborough was not bred by D.P. but by Major Holliday, and bought by D.P. as a yearling. Ridden by Gordon Richards, Aldborough had won our longest race, the Queen Alexandra Stakes at Ascot, the race which will always be associated with Brown Jack who won it six years running.

Shortly after his great victory at Doncaster, Aldborough was found one morning to be in great pain, and the veterinary surgeon diagnosed a twisted gut. Every effort was made to save his life, but in vain. He had never been sick nor sorry and it had been intended to keep him in training for another year with the Gold Cup at Ascot as his main objective. Aldborough's death was a bitter blow to D.P., and a big financial loss as his potential value as a stallion was at least £30,000, and he was not insured. Fulke Walwyn described those twenty-four hours the veterinary surgeon and trainer fought to save this horse as the worst in his life.

Basil Briscoe may have been responsible for D.P.'s purchase of Golden Miller and Insurance and for training them for all their major triumphs excepting Golden Miller's fifth Gold Cup, but Fulke Walwyn was her most successful trainer of jumpers. As already stated he trained her best stayer, Aldborough, and a number of other flat race winners. While Fulke was training her jumpers and Gordon Johnson-Houghton her flat racehorses, D.P. won more races than in any other period of her career. On several occasions Johnson-Houghton saddled three winners for her in one afternoon, and shortly before his death, early in 1952, D.P. had informed him how delighted she was at the success that they had achieved together.

Gordon Johnson-Houghton met his death in a riding accident, and although his wife Helen, twin sister of Fulke Walwyn, had forgotten more about horses and their training than most men will ever know, as a woman she was not permitted to hold a trainer's licence. In similar circumstances today Helen Johnson-Houghton would automatically have become the trainer.

As there was now no official trainer at the Blewbury stables, D.P. removed her horses to Fulke Walwyn at Lambourn, undertaking to return them to Blewbury when Mrs Johnson-Houghton had found a suitable assistant who could hold the licence. This she did when Charles Jerdein was appointed trainer two years later.

Fulke Walwyn not only trained Mont Tremblant to win the Gold Cup at Cheltenham and numerous other races, he was responsible for D.P.'s buying him and his year younger half-brother, the giant Lanveoc Poulmic. Hitherto on Charlie Rogers' recommendation D.P. bought all her jumpers in Ireland, but Fulke now suggested she direct her attention to France : on the flat the French horses had been sweeping the board, and he considered that they were breeding some pretty good jumping material as well. As the result of a visit to France he paid £4,000 for a four-year-old by Gris Perle out of Paltoquette called Mont Tremblant, and so delighted with his appearance was D.P. that she commissioned Fulke to return to France and buy his half-brother by Sirtan.

It would be no exaggeration to say that D.P. fell in love at first sight with Lanveoc Poulmic, who immediately became her favourite. Obviously she preferred quantity to quality, for Lanveoc Poulmic stood nearly a hand taller than his half-brother but lacked his symmetry. Both horses had been trained in France by Willie Head, and Mont Tremblant had won a flat race at Longchamp.

For such a big horse Lanveoc Poulmic showed incredible agility, proving himself unbeatable in races for maidens over both hurdles and fences, except on one occasion when he slipped up at the last fence with the race in his pocket. D.P. was convinced that he would prove to be the best horse she had owned since Golden Miller, but he was to fall a long way short of Mont Tremblant.

What a year 1952 was for Fulke Walwyn! He won the Gold Cup with the six-year-old Mont Tremblant (D. Dick), who was only running over fences for the fifth time and was a novice at the start of the season; he saddled D.P.'s Legal Joy (M. Scudamore) to finish second to Teal in the Grand National; and in June of that year he married Miss Catherine de Trafford, youngest daughter of Sir Humphrey de Trafford.

I place Mont Tremblant very high in the list of Gold Cup winners, and though I have dealt with the social side of his victory in another chapter I must pay tribute to the courage and ability of this young horse in the face of the worst conditions under which this great race has ever been run. It had rained almost unceasingly throughout the meeting and was still teeming down on the third day.

Having fallen in love with this really beautiful chestnut horse when watching him win the Coventry Handicap Chase at Kempton on D.P.'s birthday (21 February), I had made him my nap and was told I was mad to select so young and immature a horse against such seasoned performers as Grand National winner Freebooter, ESB, Greenogue and the Irish-trained Knock Hard. Freebooter fell at the eighth fence, and when they came to the second last fence there were only two in it, Mont Tremblant and Knock Hard – and Knock Hard fell.

All Mont Tremblant had to do was to pop over the last fence at his leisure, but he very nearly didn't. He hit it so hard that Dave Dick shot into the air. Mont Tremblant, however, was quite unperturbed and went on to win by ten lengths.

ESB fell at the last fence, otherwise he might have been second. I regard this performance on the part of Mont Tremblant as equal in merit to Golden Miller's first Gold Cup victory at the same age. History was nearly repeated the following year when Mont Tremblant finished second in the Grand National under 12.5, 3 lb more than Golden Miller had carried to victory nineteen years earlier.

That glorious slog to victory, through inches of mud over 3¼ miles at the age of six, took its toll of Mont Tremblant. On his return to Lambourn he was found to have strained a tendon which was to plague him for the remainder of his career; he also developed sinus trouble necessitating an operation, so one way and another was a pretty sick horse in the summer of 1952.

Mont Tremblant's good recovery seemed complete when he reappeared in the autumn. But that tendon continued to trouble him from time to time, and he was found to be lame after failing with long odds laid on him in one of his preliminary races for his second Gold Cup. His trainer therefore had been unable to give him all the work he would have liked to do before sending him to Cheltenham and in the Gold Cup he could only finish fourth to Knock Hard, Halloween and Galloway Braes. In the circumstances Fulke was well satisfied with his performance and had no doubt that, had he been fully wound-up, he would have repeated his success of the previous year. Obviously the race had been of great benefit, for his tendon was no longer a problem, and in Fulke's opinion he was a better horse than ever before when he went to Aintree to run in the Grand National. And what a marvellous race he ran with 12.5 in the saddle to finish second, beaten by four lengths by the Irish-trained Early Mist, ridden by Bryan Marshall to whom he was conceding 17 lb. 12.5 is a crushing weight round Liverpool, and Fulke Walwyn and others who have won the Grand National have assured me that every pound over twelve stone represents at least four lengths in distance. Mont Tremblant, therefore, was giving a start of sixty-eight lengths to the winner. Golden Miller had rightly been given a hero's welcome after winning the Grand National under 12.2, but I believe that Mont Tremblant put up an equally fine performance when finishing second with 3 lb more in the saddle.

Bryan Marshall had been D.P.'s jockey for several years until a series of rows resulted in her engaging Dave Dick, though Marshall continued to ride for other owners in the the Walwyn stable. I know Fulke Walwyn will agree with me that we have never seen a better steeplechase jockey than Bryan Marshall, but he will be forced to admit that his jockey was caught napping on Lanveoc Poulmic in a race at Sandown. The race was as good as over with Lanveoc Poulmic winning in a hack canter, but Bryan did not hear the warning shouts of the crowd as a horse called Daytime bore down on him, with the result that Lanveoc Poulmic was pipped at the post.

The stewards fined Bryan £25, but her horse's defeat cost D.P. rather more than that; in fact she described it as a 'double banco', and I shudder to think what that added up to. In the ordinary way she was a very philosophical loser, but she told poor Bryan, who was well aware that he had been caught napping, that he was guilty of criminal negligence.

D.P.'s resentment at Lanveoc Poulmic's exasperating defeat would not have been so great had he not been her favourite horse. She was accustomed to losing five-figure bets, and she had been racing long enough to appreciate that sometime or other in his career a jockey will throw a race away through over confidence.

There is an old saying in racing, 'The bigger he is the more there is to go wrong'. I don't entirely go along with this, but the task of supporting the massive frame of a horse such as Lanveoc Poulmic imposes a terrific strain on the animal's legs, and nine times out of ten they will give his trainer some sleepless nights. Lanveoc Poulmic was no exception. He was, however, D.P.'s *beau idéal*, and I had never seen her so demonstrative to man or beast as she was to her favourite after he had won a race at Sandown.

One cannot write off as a failure a horse who wins eleven races in the space of three seasons, but nevertheless Lanveoc Poulmic failed to realize expectations, for he never won a race of importance, and fell in the Gold Cup, in which his half-brother finished fourth. Instead of improving with maturity, he deteriorated till in his fourth season he jumped like a horse which had never seen a fence before in its life. He fell on several occasions and on others he made such bad mistakes that his jockey had to pull him up. It was evident that his legs were hurting him, and he was fired.

D.P. sent him to be trained in Ireland by Vincent O'Brien, and after a long rest he appeared to be sound, though in a letter to D.P. O'Brien described him as far from easy to train in that he took a 'terrible hold'. He was, however, fit enough to run in a race at Naas as a preliminary to the King George VI Chase at Kempton on Boxing Day. With two fences to jump Lanveoc Poulmic looked like coming home alone and storming into favour for the big Kempton race. Then that huge stride faltered, but Dave Dick could not pull him up until he had jumped the next fence. Vincent O'Brien wrote to D.P., 'He broke down so badly that we had to put him down right away. It was very, very sad.'

Some time before the expensive Lanveoc Poulmic defeat at Sandown D.P. had found fault with Bryan's riding of Prince of Denmark. Fulke thought his jockey had ridden a perfect race in an endeavour to give two stone to a very useful horse called Frere Jean, and said as much to D.P. who replied, 'I can only conclude that you and Bryan are in it together.' Fulke Walwyn is not the sort of man who will accept accusations of this nature, even if they are made in the heat of the moment by the richest woman in the world and he replied, 'If that's what you think, you know where you can put your horses, all thirty-five of them – and I've no doubt there'll be plenty of room for them.'

After such an altercation with any other trainer D.P.'s horses would have been on the move again, but Fulke's stable was on the crest of a wave, and so far from seeking a new trainer she wired 'Romeo' Rogers to send over a couple more horses from Ireland to be trained by Fulke at Lambourn. So once again everything in the garden was lovely – for the time being.

One of D.P.'s many superstitions was that her birthday was not a propitious day on which to launch a major offensive on the bookmakers. So when Fulke told her that she could have a banco on 21 February in two consecutive races on Mont Tremblant and Lanveoc Poulmic she needed a deal of persuading. Fulke was fortunately able to convince her that these half-brothers would win no matter what day it was, and when they both obliged she described it as the best birthday in her whole life. Before it she sent the following message to her head cook: 'Usual cake Monday midnight, chocolate icing ordinary white inside, layers of jam one enormous candle red for luck and 51 small ones if you can get them on.'

Prince of Denmark was one of those horses which don't know how to run a bad race and are equally happy over fences and hurdles. He seldom let his owner down when she had a banco on him and year after year he showed her a handsome profit.

Of all the jockeys who rode for D.P. the one who endeared himself to her most was Dave Dick. She liked him for his devil-may-care attitude to life, and because he was prepared to talk to her about her horses by the hour. But first and foremost she knew him to be a great jockey. Dave regarded D.P.

in much the same way as he faced up to Bechers and the Chair, formidable but nothing to get worried about.

Riding Prince of Denmark in a hurdle race at Cheltenham on 12 November 1952, Dave sustained a grievous and wholly unnecessary accident which put him out of action for nearly four months, during which time Dick Francis substituted for him on Mont Tremblant while Fred Winter rode a number of D.P.'s other horses. When racing on the inside, Dave's leg came in contact with a bar which protruded from the running rails. The bone of his left leg was smashed and the calf badly lacerated.

This was an occasion when D.P. revealed the compassion she usually kept so carefully hidden beneath layers of apparent indifference towards her fellow humans. Her sympathy for her injured jockey was only equalled by her fury at the Cheltenham executives for their carelessness, and what she described as their criminal disregard for the safety of the men whose job it was to ride round their track. Nothing was too good for Dave Dick, lying in hospital for a month before he was allowed to go home on crutches. Telephone messages were relayed by her staff to the hospital several times a day. Vanloads from Fortnum and Mason were delivered daily. If Dave had consumed all the good things which were dispatched to him by the sympathetic owner he would have weighed fourteen stone by the time he was discharged from hospital.

With D.P.'s full support, Dave Dick brought an action against the Cheltenham Authority for damages for injuries caused by their negligence. The case was settled out of court to the plaintiff's satisfaction.

Only the very few who knew D.P. well realized the sympathy and compassion she stored away for those in need of help. I have already described her long association with the Russian Home. What a tragedy it was that D.P. could only show her love of people when they were suffering some physical disability, and that she could not find it in her heart to share in their joys.

81

Her attitude to her horses was similar. She seldom, if ever, visited them in their stables, and more often than not arrived too late to see her runners in the paddock before a race; she would lead in her important winners, but took little interest in those which finished unplaced. On the other hand, if a horse of hers met with an accident in the course of a race she was genuinely distressed. She had no great love for horses as such, but a real affection for certain individual animals.

1954 was a tragic year for her. Legal Joy was so badly injured in the Grand National that he had to be put down in full view of the stands, and a few weeks later her brilliant young chaser Glenbeigh dropped dead from an internal haemorrhage after running in a race at Cheltenham. D.P. had formed an affection for this young horse which seemed destined for fame in the near future, and knowing how distressed she would be Fulke and Cath Walwyn decided not to tell her till the following day. But some busybody broke the news to her and the Walwyns received no thanks for their endeavour to spare her feelings.

In his first season with D.P. Fulke Walwyn was leading trainer with sixty winners and £11,115 in stakes, and D.P. was second in the list of winning owners, sixteen of her horses having won twenty-eight races, £5,665 in stakes. The leading owner was Mr McDowell, whose solitary success was with Caughoo, the 100–1 winner of the Grand National, value £11,125.

Fulke's achievement made history, as he was the first trainer to head the list without winning the Grand National, at that time almost four times more valuable than any other race. Fulke repeated this performance the following season and D.P. was again second in the list of leading owners. Mr Proctor, whose Sheila's Cottage, trained by Neville Crump, won the Grand National won £9,801 against D.P.'s £8,246 – representing forty successes by twenty-one horses. Fulke broke all previous records for races won, forty of his horses having won seventy-five races, value £16,790. His most successful horse was Mr A. G. Boley's Roland Roy whose success in the King George VI Stakes netted £2,256.

Jack Tatters and Happy Home won four races for D.P., and Happy Home was second in the Gold Cup. In 1949, for the third year running D.P. finished second in the list of winning owners with forty-two winners and £8,375 in stakes. Fulke finished top of the list of winning trainers with thirty-six winners of sixty-four races, value £15,563.

Those prolific money-spinners Jack Tatters and Prince of Denmark each won five races for D.P. Stake money was still very small compared with the prizes that are won today, and D.P.'s most valuable prize was £688 for the Sandown Park Open Chase won by Jack Tatters. Prince of Denmark's five successes brought in only £102 each, while Happy Home's solitary success was in a race worth £136. In 1950 D.P. won £5,207 on the flat with Aldborough, Angelico and River Tay the chief subscribers – in the previous jumping season Aldborough had won three hurdle races, value £715. In 1951 D.P. was third in the list of winning owners, with thirty-nine successes, value £7,414, and Fulke third in the trainers list with fifty-nine successes, value £11,739.

By the end of 1951 Fulke Walwyn had trained 186 winners for D.P. I have described 1952 as his great year. It was also a great year for D.P. who, with £14,191, was leading owner, nineteen of her horses having won fifty races. Telegram won seven hurdle races including the Coronation Hurdle at Liverpool and the Tudor Rose Hurdle at Hurst Park. He was unlucky to be born in the same year as Sir Ken. After the death of Gordon Johnson-Houghton, Fulke Walwyn took over twenty-eight of D.P.'s flat racehorses, and in the seasons 1952–3 he saddled fifty-four winners on the flat, fifty-two of them in the colours of D.P. In 1952 he trained a brilliant two-year-old filly for D.P. called Wilna, who had the rare distinction of winning both the Errol Stakes at Ascot and the Molecombe Stakes at Goodwood by the wide margin of eight lengths. Wilna had to have some give in the ground and Fulke, having taken her to Salisbury and told D.P. that she could have a double banco, discovered that the going was too firm to risk running a filly of whom he had the highest hopes. This view was shared by Gordon Richards, who was to ride her.

The going at Salisbury is very seldom firm, but this meeting took place towards the end of a long drought. D.P., however, was persuaded by Mrs Allwright, her close friend and former secretary, that conditions were perfect. Mrs Allwright, who had very little knowledge of racing, explained that she had walked part of the course in five-inch heels, and that as they had made a visible imprint it would be perfectly safe to run Wilna. Fulke Walwyn, however, made it perfectly clear that in his view Mrs Allwright was all wrong, and that if D.P. insisted on running this very valuable filly on going which might jeopardize her whole career she could find someone else to train her. D.P. therefore gave a grudging, 'You win', and walked off with Mrs A. who was protesting loudly at what she described as 'weak-kneed capitulation'.

D.P. had intended leaving immediately for Hermits Wood after Wilna's race as she had no other runner, but Mrs A. insisted that having made the journey from Chalfont St Giles they should see the programme through, and D.P. agreed. Invariably she embarked on a large meal on her return from racing, and she had ordered an outsize dish of vegetables to be ready for her at 4 p.m. When she agreed to stay on for a few more races she sent a telegram to her head cook, 'Retard vegetables one hour,' and when she agreed to remain for the last race she sent another telegram, 'Retard vegetables further hour, if ruined, cook second supply.'

Disappointed over Wilna, and bored to death at the prospect of watching five races in which she had no runner of her own, D.P. decided to go to town on other people's horses, something she rarely did unless she thought she knew something. The result was disastrous. Sir Francis Cassel told Fulke Walwyn, 'She betted like a drunken sailor and lost £25,000 in bets I did for her. God knows how much she lost with other people.'

No two men could have been more dissimilar than Sir Francis Cassel and Fulke Walwyn, but they got on extremely well. Cassel understood racing, and Fulke who is one hundred per cent professional, appreciated this. The people who infuriate him are those who don't know which end a horse kicks with, but consider themselves entitled to air their views on the subject of racing. A mutual affection existed between D.P. and the Walwyns, and she used to describe them as 'my kind of people', which was the highest praise she could bestow on anyone. In another part of this story I have reported how D.P.'s messages to Sir Francis were often very curt and always to the point. I have none of his answers in my possession, but Fulke Walwyn informed me that Sir Francis was quite able to care for himself.

During the eight seasons Fulke Walwyn trained for D.P. she only once visited her horses, but on one memorable occasion she went back to Saxon House for a late tea after attending a nearby horse show. This was a very gracious act on her part, as her usual custom when paying one of her rare visits to the homes of her acquaintances was to take her own food and thermos flask of tea with her and consume them in the car outside the front door. On this occasion, what was intended to be a brief meal developed into a party, and it was 6.30 the following morning when D.P. set off to drive herself back to Hermits Wood.

D.P. occasionally asked the Walwyns to accompany her to a theatre, but they always took the precaution of saying they would meet her at the theatre if she would give them the numbers of the seats. On one occasion she had taken the stage box into which she rushed breathless just as the cast were taking their final bow. To the accompaniment of the strains of the National Anthem she demanded at the top of her voice, 'What was it like? Was it any good? Should I have enjoyed it?' She always asked the same question half a dozen times and seldom waited for an answer.

1953–4 was another fine season for D.P. and Walwyn, who both finished second in their respective lists: D.P. won twenty-eight races, value £7,702 and Fulke, fifty races, value £12,833. Of the three races Mont Tremblant took, the most valuable was the Grand International Chase at Sandown, worth £1,068, a great performance as he was giving 3 lb to Halloween and yet beat him by six and a half lengths. But the sands were running out for D.P. In the 1954–5 season she dropped to eleventh place with only ten races won, value £2,153.

On one occasion when the combination was on the crest of the wave D.P. said to Fulke, 'When we eventually part company, as we undoubtedly shall, let's do it quietly and with dignity, no shouting at one another and no statements to the Press.' So when Fulke Walwyn felt that the end was in sight he asked her very tactfully, one day when they were alone together, whether she did not think that some other trainer might not get better results with the horses she now owned, and if so would not the end of the season be a good time to make the change. D.P. agreed, and that summer her horses went to be trained by 'Frenchy' Nicholson, who had ridden Golden Miller in that final Gold Cup which he did not win.

11

The story of Nucleus

Fulke Walwyn trained 365 winners for D.P., which may not be a record but was a tremendous achievement in the course of eight seasons. His greatest days, however, had yet to come, and two years after D.P.'s horses left his stable he set up a fresh record by winning £23,013 for his patrons. Mandarin, Taxidermist and Mill House are just three of the great horses trained at Saxon House, Lambourn, who subsequently won great steeplechases, and in 1964 he achieved his only remaining ambition – to win the Grand National which he had won as an amateur rider on Reynoldstown in 1936. The horse was Team Spirit, the smallest horse in the field, who, ridden by Willie Robinson, came from out of the clouds to achieve the apparently impossible and compensate Walwyn for the narrow defeats of Legal Joy and Mont Tremblant in the colours of D.P. in 1952 and 1953.

D.P.'s chasing fortunes were now at a low ebb. 'Romeo' Rogers's seemingly never-ending supply of potential winners from Ireland had at last dried up, and D.P. refused to allow Fulke Walwyn to look elsewhere for promising material, though it was only a few years earlier that he had gone to France and returned with Mont Tremblant and Lanvecc Poulmic. D.P.'s apparently inexhaustible energy was on the wane, probably the result of her ever-increasing weight (she still declined to mount the scales but had she done so I have no doubt they would have registered over twenty stone). She had long ceased to visit her training stables, had not been to Ireland since the war and now went racing less and less, only consenting to do so if her trainer assured her that she had a good chance of winning at least two races.

D.P. in the old days would buy any horse that seemed likely to win her a race, but now she fiddled while Rome burned, after her sensational success of the past seven seasons, apparently unable to appreciate that once-great horses were no longer great and that those which should have taken their place were no good. She grumbled when week after week passed without her trainer telling her she could have a banco, and it is a fact that the compulsive gambler will lose sooner than have no bet.

Fulke Walwyn has trained so many horses of outstanding merit that I wondered whether my idea of the best horse he has had in his stable coincided with his; it did – the horse's name was Mont Tremblant. Mandarin, whom he trained for Madame Hennessey, was a marvel, and his victory in the Grand Steeplechase de Paris, ridden by Fred Winter and with a broken bridle, was a miraculous achievement, but Fulke gives pride of place to Mont Tremblant by reason of the fact that Mandarin never carried 12.5 into second place in the Grand National. He regards this performance by D.P.'s horse as the outstanding achievement by a steeplechaser in his long experience.

Fulke Walwyn has been described to me by John (Taxidermist) Oaksey as the greatest jumping trainer of all time, and none is in a better position to judge than he. I personally have no inclination to disagree with him. Only two other men, to my knowledge, have trained and ridden the winner of the Grand National – the Hon. Aubrey Hastings, who trained and rode Prince Hartyfeldt's Ascetic's Silver to secure it in 1906, and eighteen years later trained Master Robert to win for Lord Airlie; and Fred Winter, who as a jockey won the Grand National on Sundew in 1957, on Kilmore in 1962 and later trained Jay Trump to win in 1965 and Anglo in 1966.

At no time in the course of her career as an owner of race-horses did D.P. enjoy success on the flat comparable with that which came her way over jumps. Though Fulke Walwyn and his brother-in-law Gordon Johnson-Houghton saddled a flock of winners for her under Jockey Club rules in the late forties and early fifties the majority of them were in races of minor importance.

In 1955, however, she owned in Nucleus a three-year-old son of Derby-winner Nimbus and the Blandford mare Angelus, whom she had bred herself and who was probably the best flat racehorse ever to carry her colours. Charles Jerdein, who was now the licensed trainer at Blewbury, realized that Nucleus was not forward enough to shine as a two-year-old, but nevertheless ran him three times to teach him his business. Nucleus wintered well, and after a home gallop early in April, Jerdein and Helen Johnson-Houghton informed a delighted D.P. that she could have a double banco on him when he made his three-year-old debut in a maiden race at Wolverhampton. Ridden by Lester Piggott, Nucleus started at 6–4 on and won by four lengths.

In his next race, the Two Thousand Guineas, a very high aim with so inexperienced a horse, he failed to finish in the first dozen. As he started at 66–1 one can assume that D.P. had little fancy for him but he won four of his seven subsequent races and finished second in the other three.

Following his race in the first classic he carried a 7 lb penalty to a six lengths victory at Windsor, landing a second banco for his owner at 5–4 on, after this won a good class 1¼ miles handicap at Hurst Park under top weight by four lengths at 9–4 (another banco), and in late June at Birmingham he ran a magnificent race to finish second to Tamerlane, beaten 1½ lengths, at a difference of only 4 lb. Tamerlane had started favourite for the Two Thousand Guineas, in which he was beaten a neck by Our Babu.

Ridden by Lester Piggott, Nucleus confirmed his right to be considered among the best classic colts of his year by winning the King Edward VII Stakes, value £5,186, at Royal

Ascot by three lengths from True Cavalier in the style of a real stayer. Next to Straight Deal's Derby this was the most important three-year-old event won by D.P., and incidentally, more valuable than her wartime classic.

In the Gordon Stakes at Goodwood, with odds of 5–2 freely bet on him, Nucleus was beaten four lengths by the moderate Manati, giving the impression that he might have taken a dislike to racing, but he ran a magnificent race in the St Leger when running the peerless Meld to three-quarters of a length. Admittedly, Meld was running a temperature, and sickening for the cough which was rampant that autumn, but Nucleus would have won the final classic by three lengths had she not been in the field, and must be given credit for a splendid performance.

Lester Piggott lodged an objection against Harry Carr for crossing, but no one took it very seriously except the stewards who kept Lester's tenner, having very swiftly overruled his complaint. Nucleus wound up the season by winning the Jockey Club Stakes, value £4,765. Lester rode him very tenderly, and Nucleus did all he had to do without extending himself, but I got the impression that he was not enjoying himself and that had his jockey moved on him he might have capitulated. It was decided, however, to send him over to the States to run in the Washington International, and D.P. sent a secretary to London Airport to report on every detail of his embarkation for Maryland on a Pan American plane, together with Darius, Prefect and the Irish-trained Pana-slipper. The report runs to three pages.

Had any bookmaker offered 500–1 against D.P.'s accepting any one of the dozens of offers of hospitality which reached her from the United States when it was known that Nucleus was to run at Laurel Park, they would have been guilty of pinching the odds. Her cousins, the Whitneys, were naturally anxious to entertain her, but the bulk of the invitations were from strangers. Americans have always evinced a passionate interest in the unusual, and stories of D.P.'s eccentricities had spread far and wide across the western hemisphere.

Many of these were fabrications, while others were gross exaggerations, but the presence of the Hon. Dorothy Wyndham Paget, owner of Nucleus, one of the favourites for the Washington International, would have excited the interest of the masses in the same way as did the bearded lady, the two-headed monster, and the smallest dwarf in creation.

To D.P., however, a far bigger burden than her notoriety would have been the kindly people who wanted to entertain her, literally hundreds of them, all crowding round her, anxious to shake her by the hand. If there was one thing D.P. hated above all it was other people's parties, and in Maryland, famed for its hospitality, she would not have been allowed to remain in her car outside her host's house, and be supplied with boiling water with which to make her own tea, whilst she ate her own sandwiches and her own legs of chicken (with her fingers). There would have been people everywhere, and, worst of all, a preponderence of men, all trying to get as close to her as possible.

Anyway, she did not go, and would learn the result at home in Hermits Wood, Chalfont St Giles.

On his form in the St Leger, Nucleus was a worthy representative of this country, as was Darius, who had won the previous year's Two Thousand Guineas and the Eclipse Stakes and finished third in the Derby, but both horses ran atrociously, Darius finishing ninth and Nucleus last. The race was won by El Chama from Venezuela by a head from another Venezuelan horse Prendase, with the American horse Social Outcast third and Panaslipper fourth. The result was a tremendous surprise to racegoers all over the world, probably including Venezuela, as the Venezuelan horses had never been considered to be in the same class as those trained in Europe and the United States.

D.P. heard the news in an exclusive Transatlantic telephone broadcast. To Chalfont St Giles, Buckinghamshire 208, from Parkway, Maryland 50400, came the call – a quarter past nine in night-shrouded England; 4.15 p.m. on Laurel Park racecourse. It was Mr John D. Schapiro, the Laurel Park

President, who was speaking from his air-conditioned room on the top of the new £1 million clubhouse. The room was crowded with guests from all over the world sitting in their armchairs, waiting for the start of this £23,000 international race. As the thirteen runners approached the start, Mr Schapiro said: 'We all here wish you the best of luck in your sporting action. Now Miss Paget, I am going to hand you over to Clive Graham of the *Daily Express*, who has a telephone beside him in the Press Box and who will describe the race for you.'

The telephone rang and Miss Paget heard: 'Hello, this is Clive Graham.' When it became apparent that Nucleus had no chance of winning, but had every chance of finishing last, Clive must have wished that he had not accepted this job, but D.P. was a wonderful loser and thanked him most courteously for giving her a first-hand description of the race.

As a four-year-old, Nucleus soon revealed that his form in the United States the previous autumn was all wrong. In winning the Paradise Stakes of 1¾ miles at Hurst Park by three-quarters of a length from the smart Daemon he proved that his close second to Meld in the St Leger, over a similar distance, had been no fluke. Next time out at Kempton he won the Victor Wild Stakes and followed this up by proving himself the best four-year-old stayer by beating Lord Derby's Acropolis in the Winston Churchill Stakes of 2 miles 70 yards. This was a tremendous performance, and one which gave Nucleus a favourite's chance in the Gold Cup at Ascot. At the beginning of June, however, he became desperately ill, tumour on the brain was suspected, and as his condition deteriorated Charles Jerdein decided that the most humane course was to put him down. The death of Nucleus was a tragic loss for D.P., as apart from his outstanding prospects in the Cup Races his potential value as a stallion was at least £200,000. D.P., so far as I know, never insured her horses, and Nucleus was no exception.

Twice in his career Nucleus had run unaccountably badly, and there were those who suspected his courage, but it is possibly that he was already subject to spasmodic attacks of the malady which led to his death. Though he did not run in the Derby as he was still judged backward in the June of his three-year-old career, I rate Nucleus a better horse than Straight Deal: his performance in the St Leger was superior in my opinion to anything Straight Deal accomplished, while his three victories as a four-year-old established him as a champion.

12

'We shall miss her'

Basil Briscoe once said: 'Training Dorothy Paget's horses is child's play, but it's a hell of a bloody job trying to train D.P.' Since those faraway days a dozen men had expressed these sentiments, though maybe not in those exact words. Now, at long last, the great ship had sailed into calm water, and with Sir Gordon Richards and 'Frenchy' Nicholson, who were still training for her at the time of her death, she never had a difference of opinion.

It had taken a full season for D.P. to realize that she no longer owned horses of the calibre of Nucleus and Mont Tremblant, but when she accepted that the great days were over, at any rate for the present, she instructed her trainers to win as many races as possible with the material at their disposal. This meant that they should run her horses against those of their own class, or even stoop to conquer against the most lowly opposition. They were definitely not to be aimed at the big prizes.

Many years ago, an old-timer Newmarket trainer remarked to me, 'The trouble with my guvnor is that he will think his Yarmouth bloaters are Ascot salmon.' It has always been the policy of Newmarket trainers to run the least distinguished members of their stables at Yarmouth, while the élite went to Ascot. D.P. had never been one of those owners who insist that a two-year-old which has scrambled home in a maiden race at Wolverhampton on a Tuesday in April should next

run in the Coventry Stakes at Ascot. The only occasion in
which I can recall D.P. running one of her horses out of its
class was when she ran Tuppence in the Derby; she was
young at the time and thought it would be fun to see her
colours carried in our premier race, but she did not have a
penny on him.

Once D.P. got used to the idea that her horses were second-
rate, she realized that little fish can be sweet, and the bigger
the bet you land with them, the sweeter the fish. In the
evening of her life, D.P. became increasingly lethargic
physically and went racing only if Sir Gordon or 'Frenchy'
could promise her two bancos. But with horses in England
being put to jumping more often, though 'Frenchy' placed
her horses very astutely, the days on which he and his wife
could tell D.P. that she was reasonably sure to win two races
were few and far between.

D.P. now seldom left Hermits Wood without Mrs A., and
one day she agreed to visit her parents on the way back from
a race meeting. As D.P. loathed meeting strangers, and went
to great lengths to avoid doing so, this was a tremendous
feather in Mrs A.'s cap, but did not increase her popularity
with the other members of the Hermits Wood household.
Olili was on friendly terms with Mrs A., but three are a
crowd, and when Mrs A. was a member of the trio she could
make it seem like a mob. From time to time, without any loss
of dignity, Olili was able to hold her own by conversing with
D.P. in French, which Mrs A. did not understand. It appealed
to D.P.'s impish sense of fun to exclude Mrs A. from the
conversation in this way, which she called 'sending Barbara
to Coventry'. Olili was trilingual (French, English and German), and as her mother was Russian she may have spoken
that language as well. D.P. had spoken fluent French when
she returned to England from Princess Mestchersky's school
in Paris at the age of eighteen, and though she seldom went
to Paris after the closure of the Russian Home she was still
able to carry on a French conversation with Olili, the course
of which evidently frustrated Mrs A.

D.P.'s physical lethargy did not extend to her mind, which remained extremely active, and her notes and telephone calls increased with her tendency to stay at home, imposing an even greater strain on her secretaries. Never in the course of racing history has so much energy been expended in the production of so little.

D.P. had first made up her mind to train with Gordon Richards on the day in June 1939 when he made her laugh after Colonel Payne had cost her several fortunes, by anyone else's standards, in finishing unplaced in the Cork and Orrery Stakes. Even if a man is a knight and has been champion jockey twenty-six times he enters on a new profession with a certain degree of trepidation. Sir Gordon has told me that owners were not exactly falling over one another to send him horses when he received the message from D.P. saying she would like him to train for her, a request to which he readily agreed.

D.P. was anxious that her new trainer should start his career with a winner, but this seemed unlikely as his horses were somewhat backward. However, she had a two-year-old called The Saint, trained by 'Romeo' Rogers in Ireland, which 'Romeo' had galloped good enough to win any maiden race in the course of the first couple of months of the season. She, therefore, instructed Rogers to send The Saint over to Sir Gordon's stables, while at the same time she entered him for a two-year-old race at Windsor, 'one of my lucky courses'. D.P. had always preferred the minor meetings to the more fashionable affairs at which she had to discard her old 'speckled hen' coat in favour of some more conventional attire, thus Royal Ascot was anathema to her, and although she owned a box she only put in an appearance when she had a runner, usually leaving as soon as its race was over.

Her two favourite meetings were Windsor and Folkestone and she had more bancos on these courses than on any others. The opposition was seldom very strong, and she would bet in thousands on her runners, which almost invariably started at odds on. On one occasion when she sent a filly from

'Frenchy' Nicholson

Centre Tuppence, one of D.P.'s early disappointments

Below Colonel Payne, another bad investment

Above The famous
Golden Miller,
G. Wilson up

Opposite above
Straight Deal with
T. Carey up. Trainer
Walter Nightingall
holds the horse

Opposite below
Lanveoc Poulmic,
D. Dick up

Left Insurance

Mont Tremblant, D. Dick up

Aggie (right), who became companion to Golden Miller in his retirement, pictured with another friend

Ireland called Albany Blue to run in a Folkestone selling race, value £100, she romped home at 6–1 on, and D.P. had to go to 860 guineas to buy the horse in. One wonders how much D.P. had on her winner to make the transaction worthwhile. The following week Albany Blue won a much better-class race at Windsor just as easily as she won the selling race.

The Saint arrived at Sir Gordon's place a week before he was due to run at Windsor, and D.P. and her retinue arrived at Windsor in time to see him in the paddock. Ridden by Jock Wilson, The Saint carried one of D.P.'s double bancos, and proved himself well up to the task by winning with his ears pricked. I have seldom seen D.P. demonstrate her delight in such tangible form; champagne flowed and everyone wanted to congratulate Sir Gordon on starting his new career with a winner. Sir Gordon, however, disclaimed all credit for The Saint's victory, and pointed to Rogers, who had come over from Ireland to witness his triumph, saying 'That's the fella who's done all the work.' D.P. was not in the habit of publicly celebrating the victories of her horses, but she made an exception in this case as it constituted a happy augury for the future of Sir Gordon Richards in his new profession.

D.P. was even more superstitious on racecourses than she was at home. Some places and some loos were lucky, while others were the kiss of death. Because of The Saint's success any place on which she had stood or sat on that momentous occasion was lucky, and I have copies of messages to Sir Francis, her trainer and members of her staff to meet her at the same table in the restaurant that she had occupied on the day that The Saint won. Since at the end of her life she went racing only if she could have two bancos, if the first horse won she would instruct the trainer to meet her on exactly the same spot in the paddock before the second one was due to run.

As she now owned no horses of outstanding merit she was more obsessed than ever before with betting and she did not care at what price her horses started so long as she could have a banco. Occasionally Sir Gordon would say 'I think we might win a very nice race with so and so,' to which she would reply, 'Nice race my foot, we'll run him at Folkestone and Windsor.' The size of her bet depended on how much Sir Gordon was prepared to risk of his own money. If he said he wanted a tenner on she would say, 'If that's the case I'll only have a tiddler,' which I assume was somewhere around £300. If Sir Gordon said, 'I want a "pony" (£25),' she would have a banco. While if he declared he was going to risk £50, which was his limit, her countenance would light up with a beaming smile and she would have a double banco. All Sir Gordon's bets were included in D.P.'s and she sent him a cheque or a bill as the case might be on the day after the end of each flat racing season.

Moderate horses require more astute placing than their more distinguished fellows. Until recently a horse such as Mont Tremblant to all intents and purposes made his own entries. The Gold Cup would be his main objective and if he was none the worse for that race he would run in the Grand National. Prior to Cheltenham he would run in four or five races in which the opposition was preferably not too severe; but since D.P.'s day the sponsors have intervened in a big way, and there is now a far wider selection of rich steeplechases to be won.

D.P. was never happier than when poring over the Racing Calendar and thumbing through form books to ascertain the most propitious races in which to run her second-rate horses, who were giving her a great deal of enjoyment, though she seldom saw them run. Making entries presented no problem to D.P. as she entered half a dozen horses in every race in which they were eligible to run, but the selection of which of their many engagements they should fulfil required hours of study and a vast number of telephone messages to be relayed by her secretaries to her trainers.

Sir Gordon had ridden for D.P. for approximately eighteen years, and in 1952 and 1953, when Fulke Walwyn trained her flat racehorses, Sir Gordon and Scobie Breasley rode a large proportion of her winners. A mutual affection existed between

them and when D.P. made some more than usually outrageous statement or suggestion Sir Gordon would smile and
say, looking her straight in the eye, 'Miss Paget, you know
you don't really mean that.' D.P. would laugh and agree that
she didn't.

D.P. also had a warm regard for Scobie Breasley, whom she
always referred to as 'that miserable Breasley'. The reason for
this apparently unflattering reference to the stable jockey was
because 'he frightens the wits out of me when I've got a
banco.' If Harry Wragg was the Head Waiter Scobie was the
Maitre d'Hotel. No matter whether the race was over five
furlongs or 2¾ miles Scobie would drop his mount out in the
early stages of a race in order to give it plenty of time to find
its stride, and when D.P. had a double banco she went
through agony while with only a furlong to go the medium
of her gamble still had a length or two to make up. But Scobie
was a consummate artist at judging the exact moment at
which to make his effort, and more often than not it was only
in the last fifty yards that his mount would draw smoothly
into the lead to land D.P. her banco.

There were never two jockeys more dissimilar than Sir
Gordon and Scobie, but Sir Gordon had the highest opinion
of a man who was his jockey for ten years, and of whom he
once said to me, 'No matter how close the finish may have
been you've still got a horse if it's been ridden by Scobie, and
nine times out of ten it will be all the better for the race.'

D.P. too had the highest opinion of Scobie's skill, but on
several occasions when they were in the parade ring and
Scobie was about to mount some horse on which she had a
banco she would ask him not to leave it quite so late as he
had done last time out of consideration for her nerves.
Sir Gordon would invariably chip in with 'Don't take any
notice of her Scobie, just ride your own race.' I need hardly
add that that was what Scobie did, and that half a dozen
Dorothy Pagets wouldn't have changed his style.

Evidence of D.P.'s regard for Scobie was forthcoming when
he met with a serious accident and the doctor reported that

he wouldn't be fit to ride again for at least a month. When she heard the news D.P. actually spoke on the telephone herself to Sir Gordon, instructing him not to run any of her horses till Scobie was fit to ride them again. Sir Gordon replied that while it was a wonderful gesture, her self-sacrifice would not expedite Scobie's recovery, rather the reverse as he would be horrified at the idea of Miss Paget's withdrawing her horses from races in which they had good chances of winning. D.P. agreed that her suggestion would serve no good purpose but she kept in close touch with her jockey while he was in hospital and was delighted when he won on the first horse he rode for her following his return to the saddle.

Like Sir Gordon, 'Frenchy' Nicholson had also recently retired from the saddle when D.P. engaged him as her trainer under National Hunt rules. He had been a most successful National Hunt jockey and topped the list on a number of occasions. The jumpers which came to him from Fulke Walwyn's stable were much on a par in point of merit with those Sir Gordon trained on the flat, but 'Frenchy' as a young trainer, was delighted to be sent thirty jumpers the majority of whom would be capable of winning races, and with the promise of more and better ones to come. He was determined to make full use of his good fortune and, to his credit, he succeeded.

The Nicholson stable was a family affair with 'Frenchy' as trainer, his wife Diana dealing with the vast correspondence unavoidable if you trained for D.P., while in the last two seasons of D.P.'s life their young son David was the stable jockey. Diana Nicholson is wise in the ways of human beings as well as of horses, a priceless asset with a husband training for D.P., whom she seldom met, and few days went by without her phoning a message of approximately 500 words in reply to D.P.'s questions and suggestions, containing her own suggestion as to where the horses which had been so extensively entered should run.

A few months before her death D.P. said to Sir Gordon, 'I think it's about time we went to market and acquired some new blood.' She also told the Nicholsons that she was arranging for her jumpers, trained in Ireland, to be sent over to be trained by them for the following season. There were reported to be several highly promising young chasers among them. This disproves the theory that her previous reluctance to replenish her stock of racehorses was due to a premonition that she had not long to live. Even when she had realized that her jumping stable was now only a second-rate power she believed that 'Romeo' would sooner or later produce a potential Happy Home or Roman Hackle and maybe even a Golden Miller. She was now breeding on the very best lines at Ballymacoll, so surely there should, before long, be a Straight Deal or a Nucleus among the thirty or so foals which were born every year.

Scientific mating of the best available stock will eventually produce a champion, but merit has a way of skipping a generation or two, and in order to breed a classic winner an owner must not only be well endowed with wordly goods, but also with unlimited patience. In recent years Sir Michael Sobell, who now owns the Ballymacoll stud and much of D.P.'s best female blood, is reaping the benefit of the matings which failed to provide D.P. with a horse of oustanding merit.

Mrs Nicholson told me that during the four and a half years her husband trained for D.P. she only went racing on four or five occasions. On one of these occasions she had the great pleasure of seeing her favourite old warrior Prince of Denmark, two days before his thirteenth birthday, win the Kingsclear handicap chase at Newbury carrying 11.13, with Dave Dick in the saddle at 7–2. 'The Prince', as D.P. always referred to him, had been hard at it for nearly ten years but he appeared as sprightly as ever as he sprinted away from the last fence to beat Rosenkavalier, six years his junior.

If there were more horses like Prince of Denmark everyone would want to be a trainer, but on this day he was only one of the trio to bring joy to D.P.'s heart. On the same afternoon her five-year-old Straight Lad, also ridden by Dave Dick, won the Learners Hurdle from a field of fifteen by six lengths at

13–8 on, while the three-year-old Primate, ridden by Sprague, won the Hants Maiden Hurdle by half a length at 6–4 from a field of nineteen. Even single bancos had been few and far between in the past eighteen months, and D.P. could not remember when she had last brought off a double banco, but on this great day she had won half the races on the card and had had a banco on all three of them. No wonder the Nicholsons were popular.

This was Prince of Denmark's last success, but Straight Lad was to prove himself almost as successful a money-spinner as the Prince himself. Trained by 'Frenchy' Nicholson Straight Lad won four of his five races that season, losing only at Newbury when he finished second to a very smart horse, Prince Stephen, to whom he was conceding 18 lb.

Ridden by Dave Dick, this home-bred son of Straight Deal won ten hurdle races, and on the flat took the Newbury Autumn Cup, the Spring Handicap at Liverpool, ridden in both by Manny Mercer, and the Burlington Handicap at Hurst Park in which Scobie Breasley was his jockey. The Newbury Autumn Cup over two miles was one of the few successes D.P. enjoyed in a big handicap race.

Mrs Nicholson described Straight Lad to me in the following words: 'As brave and honest as they come, I don't think he ever let us down.' Pride of Denmark, no relation to the Prince, showed great promise when winning good-class steeplechases at Newbury and Kempton, but he proved very difficult to train, though he did win a steeplechase at Kempton when running in the name of the Executors, a month after D.P.'s death.

The most successful chaser trained by Nicholson for D.P. was Pelopidas, winning seven times in all. Her last success in England was with Admiral's Lodge, ridden by David Nicholson in the Boveney Juvenile Hurdle at Windsor on 12 December 1959. Her last winner in Ireland was at Naas on 30 January 1960.

No sport, anywhere in the world, owes so much to one benefactor as National Hunt racing does to Dorothy Paget.

It is no exaggeration to say that she was largely responsible for the current popularity of jumping and for its universal recognition as being on a par with flat racing, no longer its poor and slightly disreputable relation. Had it not been for D.P.'s patronage when the sport was at a low ebb, I do not believe that sponsors today would be falling over one another to promote valuable races bearing their name. It is now hard to believe that Golden Miller's six Cheltenham Gold Cups were each worth only £670.

The flat racing community, and in particular breeders of bloodstock, also owe her a debt of gratitude. It is surprising that neither the Jockey Club nor the National Hunt Committee has perpetuated her memory by sponsoring races bearing her name as a token of their gratitude for her services to racing. It is also surprising that she did not leave a memorial to herself in the form of endowments to charitable organizations, medical research and the foundation of scholarships. I realize that had she done so it would have been out of character, but wills often turn out to be surprising documents revealing a side of the deceased's character which no one had any idea existed.

D.P.'s besetting sin was her lack of a sense of moral obligation, and her failure to make a will was in keeping with her lifelong inability to arrive at a decision and stick to it. It was, in fact, an extension of her habit of sending up fifteen horses for sale and withdrawing a dozen of them, or ordering her trainer to send a horse to run at a meeting then scratching it before it arrived at the course.

For thirty years she had indulged in no intellectual exercise, and her reading was confined to an endless flow of 'whodunnits'. In consequence, her mental apparatus had declined, and she had become a creature of impulse, who lived her life by a series of reflex actions.

Mr James de Rothschild, who also died intestate, made it clear that he had done so as a token of gratitude to the country which had given him so much happiness. If more rich men felt the same way the Chancellor of the Exchequer would be able to make a further cut in taxation. D.P., I feel sure, was not prompted by any philanthropic sentiments towards the community at large, and I think that she would eventually have got round to making a will. All her life she had cut things fine, the last appointment at the dentist, the last to cast her vote at the election, and her arrival on race-courses timed to the split second when her horse would be at the starting gate.

On this final occasion, she left it too late and missed her deadline. Of her estate, valued at £3,803,380, the Chancellor of the Exchequer appropriated all but £736,000. I know that pressure had been put upon her by a certain individual to make a will, and she is alleged to have said that she was giving it her consideration. I doubt whether she got very far with it, for not even a rough draft was found after her death among the mountains of correspondence at Hermits Wood.

I do not know the size of the fortune D.P. inherited from the Whitney family when she came of age, but it must have been considerably more than the figure at which her estate was valued at her death. I do not suggest that D.P. spent her money wisely and well, but she gave employment to hundreds and entertainment to millions, and no one knows how much of her wealth was expended in secrecy on helping those in need.

A large number of her horses were sold within a few months of her death: at one sale in Dublin thirty-two lots fetched £35,461, a number of which were jumpers, originally destined to be trained by Nicholson. For a chestnut gelding called Drumshambo Neville Crump paid 6,100 guineas; for another, Fortescue, Mr Hugh Sumner paid 6,500 guineas; and a third, Fairy Flame, fetched 2,300 guineas at the Ascot sale. Later in the year twenty-two brood mares from the Bally-macoll stud fetched 30,140 guineas at the Newmarket October Sale.

At this time it seemed likely that the entire Paget empire would be dispersed under the auctioneer's hammer, but later that year it was announced that Mr, now Sir, Michael Sobell had made a bid for the Ballymacoll stud. He trained with Sir Gordon Richards and had therefore met D.P. After consultation with Sir Gordon, Mr Sobell offered £250,000 for the stud and 130 horses, mostly brood mares and fillies. This was a most public-spirited action, and I am glad to say that it has rewarded him handsomely.

Sir Gordon has retired from training, but he has remained as racing manager to Sir Michael, whose horses are now trained by Dick Hern. These horses are the only memorial to Dorothy Paget, owner and breeder of more racehorses than any woman in the history of racing in this country. Look at the pedigree of Sir Michael's next winner, and I would like to bet that either its dam, grand-dam or great great-dam, possibly all three, once carried the colours of the Hon. Dorothy Wyndham Paget.

Many flattering obituaries appeared, with racing journalists seemingly vying with each other to make up after death for the criticisms they had heaped upon her in life. But there was one, by Len Scott, appearing in *The Sporting Life* within twenty-four hours of her death, which created a storm of controversy. I quote it in full:

The Poor Little Rich Girl

Too much money . . . too soon. An appropriate epitaph for the Hon. Dorothy Wyndham Paget. Dead at the age of fifty-four, forty-three of her years had been spent in pleasing herself. She became a millionairess at the age of eleven . . . and that was her tragedy. Poor little rich girl! That phrase might have been written for her.

Her glory? Mostly reflected. She chose the Turf as her playground and, by chance, became associated with Golden Miller, one of the greatest horses of all time. That 105 guineas yearling came to her with a £6,000 price tag around his neck, but he was the cheapest champion she would ever buy. Think of it! A Grand National and five Cheltenham Gold Cups in a row! As well as being one of the most sensational National losers ever.

Miss Paget was to pour out more than one handsome fortune as further bait to Fame, but Fame fobbed her off somewhat shabbily. Even her dream of winning a Derby was cut down to a second-class Derby, the wartime substitute affair won by Straight Deal.

So far as a woman with a reputed income of £250,000 a year can be said to have a profession, that of Miss Paget was the avoidance of publicity. She was indeed one of the first to make it an exact science (Miss Greta Garbo was a co-pioneer) and to savour all its pleasant by-products. Thus, when Miss Paget was abominably rude she lost no caste, was not written off as merely boorishly ignorant.

Miss Paget was a younger daughter of the late Lord Queenborough's first marriage – with Pauline Whitney. Pauline's father was William C. Whitney, one-time U.S. Navy Secretary and New York street-car tycoon. And when Miss Paget inherited her very considerable slice of the Whitney millions she was just eleven years old! A thin-legged, pigtailed child, she was daring, a good rider and had a talent for not making friends which was far beyond her years.

As a young woman she had ambitions as a concert-singer – and actually appeared in public a few times. Then she became bitten by the fast-car bug, racing in public under a 'Miss Wyndham' pseudonym. But to the public at large, her chief claim to fame was that of being the 'richest unmarried woman in Britain'.

The motor-racing phase flared up and died. Miss Paget gave financial backing to Captain Tim Birkin's team of Bentleys and sent her cars to Buenos Aires in 1931. Then she pulled out, £20,000 down on the transaction and, so it was rumoured, not entirely heart-whole.

Cars were out. Horses were in. In this field Miss Paget would have everything she wanted – and damn the price. Her behaviour at the sales could only be described as wild. She poured out money like water. Most people were broke in 1931 – the year of the Great Depression: Miss Paget paid 6,000 guineas for that yearling colt, who would become the notorious Tuppence. The Derby failure of 1933, he was eventually disposed of in a 'seller'. Blanding and Portema cost 9,400 guineas the pair. Sold for 740 guineas. She paid 21,000 guineas for three mares in 1933. In 1934 she laid out 9,100 guineas for Osway, who never won a race. In 1936 it was 11,500 guineas for Radiant – who won a couple of two-year-old races.

Climax ... in 1936, when Mrs Corlette Glorney missed buying a colt by Fairway – Golden Hair. Mrs Glorney had fallen off her shooting stick in the excitement, and one of Miss Paget's innumerable trainers bid the top ... 15,000 guineas. Named Colonel Payne, he won two races worth £150 apiece.

Before she won that Derby with Straight Deal, Miss Paget must have laid out a quarter of a million pounds. And – irony! – the mare which threw Straight Deal cost the owner only 1,800 guineas.

We shall remember Miss Paget for Golden Miller or, rather, Miss Paget will be remembered because of Golden Miller. Yet even this equine marvel was surrounded with argument and bickering. When Gerry Wilson came off Golden Miller at Aintree in 1935, we had the unedifying spectacle of the owner removing her horses from Basil Briscoe and sending them to Donald Snow, a cousin by marriage. It was Snow, by the way, who put up that 15,000 guineas bid for Colonel Payne!

Owen Anthony, Henri Jelliss, Walter Nightingall, Alec Law ... these are but a few of the trainers she discarded as the whim took her. Jockeys? Apart from Wilson, even Bryan Marshall knew the rough edge of her tongue when beaten on Lanveoc Poulmic in 1951.

We shall remember her as the bulky, Glastonbury-booted figure which appeared on the racecourse surrounded by a retinue of servants. We shall reminisce about her bad manners, enormous appetite and extraordinary clothes.

And we shall miss her!

My own opinion of this obituary was, and is, that it was honest but in poor taste. I quote it here because it summarizes the reputation she acquired for many people who knew nothing of her charities, her kindnesses and who were unwilling to acknowledge the debt owed to her by the racing community; and also because it gave rise to a rejoinder from Olili who, in her grief, came to the defence of her dead friend.

On 10 February a most undignified article on Miss Dorothy Paget by Len Scott appeared in your paper. No one can expect Mr Scott to know that Miss Paget did not inherit her fortune until she came of age. Nor can he know, when he says 'her profession was to avoid publicity', that the publicity Miss Paget avoided was for the innumerable charities on which she spent much of her income. Knowing this, Len Scott's 'she poured out a fortune as bait for Fame' is a strangely misplaced phrase.

He also cannot know that since Miss Paget had to cut down on helping to relieve distress she spent much time giving pleasure to people whom the world had treated none too kindly. Miss Paget won her first race on 7 June 1930 at Southwell and for the last time on 30 January 1960 at Naas. In all she won 1,532 races which I believe to be a European record and may even be a world record. She never wanted fame but she loved a good horse. In the past twenty years most of Miss Paget's horses were home-bred. Most of her mares were mated on her instructions. She had an extraordinary knowledge of pedigrees though she would say humbly, 'The experts know much more about it than I do.'

Miss Paget did not breed for sale and therefore not for quick returns, her intention being to breed horses which stayed 1½ miles. The offspring of this policy will, therefore, benefit British bloodstock for many years to come. Mr Scott also referred to some of Miss Paget's trainers. One can but presume that he takes it for granted that his readers know which trainers trained over jumps and which on the flat, and that some of them died while in charge of Miss Paget's horses. He is misinformed on the subject of the late Basil Briscoe and the 1935 Grand National.

It would not have fitted the tone of Mr Scott's article to mention that Charlie Rogers has trained for Miss Paget, and been in charge of many of her horses, also as a friend, adviser and manager for twenty-three years. I personally would be interested to know what kind of Derby Straight Deal could have won in England in 1943 or whether to Mr Scott, Gainsborough's World War I Derby victory was also second class.

Where Mr Scott is right is in saying, 'We shall miss her.'

Yours etc, Olga de Mumm.

Part II

Life at Hermits Wood

13

The ways of an eccentric

I am indebted to those who were in close attendance on the Hon. Dorothy Paget for details of life as it was lived by the chatelaine of Hermits Wood, Chalfont St Giles, over a period of twenty years. They reveal a real affection existing between D.P. and every member of her staff, scared of her though many of them were. She demanded reports on every incident which took place, and she answered the majority of these in her barely legible handwriting. I do not know the names of the authors of these reports, or for whom many of D.P.'s extensive communications were intended; moreover the correspondence between D.P. and her employees which has come into my possession represents less than a thousandth part of what was found in bundles and sacks after her death and sorted out by her oldest friend Olili de Mumm.

Miss Paget lived on the first floor of her house, Hermits Wood, and only came down and mixed with her staff at Christmas and New Year, or on special occasions such as Fireworks Night. She would, however, carry on conversations with members of her staff as she went to board one of her numerous motor cars on her way to a racecouse.

On returning home she went to her quarters in easy stages. Often she would sit for some time in her car at the front door and drink tea and chat to whoever had accompanied her. Before disembarking she directed someone to ask her chief secretary, Miss Williams, 'Has anything gone wrong?'

and would also send messages to the cook, as she was invariably hungry after a day's racing.

When she was ready to move, her accompanying secretary would have to remove each piece of luggage and show it to her at the car window before taking it in and placing it on the oak box in the front hall. When she was sitting on it she sometimes used to ask one of her secretaries to pull out the toes of her stockings in order to ease her feet after she had removed her bootees. After the luggage had been unloaded and D.P. was comfortably seated in the front hall she would begin dictating messages to all and sundry, to be typed out before the secretary went to bed, which was never before the small hours of the following day.

Whereas D.P. invariably drove herself to a race meeting or horse show, she was too fatigued to drive herself home and handed over the wheel to her secretary. In the 1950s D.P.'s car and the car following her, usually driven by Miss Clarke (O.C. motor cars and horse show secretary), travelled at somewhere between eighty and a hundred mph. In the years immediately preceding her death D.P. drove less frequently as she often felt unwell.

Having arrived home after a race meeting, D.P. would spend hours in the dining room before going upstairs and although she had been up all day she disliked going to bed in the dark. Madame Nina Djakelly, an elderly White Russian lady whose late husband had been an ambassador, Olili de Mumm and Mrs Barbara Allwright all had rooms on the same floor as D.P. Another close friend Mrs Irene Robbins, who lived in London, visited D.P. constantly and accompanied her on her various jaunts. To the majority of her friends and secretaries D.P. had allotted a colour by which she often referred to them: so that, for example, Mrs Robbins was blue, Olili was pink and Mrs Allwright was yellow.

D.P.'s staff worked in shifts throughout the twenty-four hours. Her chief cook was Mrs Hackemer, though Mrs Styche became her chief cook at night. Mary, the head day duty maid, spent much of her time cleaning D.P.'s numerous gold and silver cups which were continually on display. Miss Benton and Miss Donald were D.P.'s two personal maids, the former caring for D.P.'s clothes and taking far more interest in them than D.P. herself. Miss Benton also laid some of D.P.'s bets, and took it in turns with Miss Donald to look after the tape, which, in D.P.'s view, was the most important piece of furniture in the whole establishment. Miss Donald did little else except tear off the messages from the tape and dispatch them by a secretary to her mistress. Watching the winners come up day after day proved a temptation to bet which poor Miss Donald could not resist and consequently she lost a good deal of money.

Miss Williams, who had been with D.P. for many years, lived on the ground floor. She never accompanied D.P. on her expeditions, her duties being entirely in the office, where she was responsible for making out and signing all D.P.'s cheques and giving and receiving trainers' messages. These latter duties were so numerous that they were shared by the other secretaries who worked in the large drawing room downstairs, a pleasant room looking onto the gardens.

Junior secretaries came and went from Hermits Wood with monotonous regularity. In response to a newspaper advertisement bright-eyed girls would arrive to be interviewed by Mrs Haase at Pollards Wood Grange, where the latter ruled the secretaries with a kindly hand, and instructed them in their duties.

It was very rare for a secretary to be given the sack, but few remained for more than a month or two, having become bored with the task of making numerous copies of unnecessary messages and running pointless errands. In 1949, however, an outstandingly attractive young woman in her twenties applied for the post of secretary-cum-chauffeuse. She gave the name of Barbara Allwright and explained that she was married with a small son, and that she and her husband lived their own lives. She impressed Mrs Haase by her enthusiasm and got the job. D.P. paid little attention to the majority of her junior secretaries, and as she invariably drove herself at that time it was not Mrs Allwright's skill at the wheel which first attracted the notice of her mistress.

Within a matter of weeks, however, they were inseparable companions and Mrs Allwright had been promoted from the secretaries' quarters at Pollards Wood Grange to a room next to D.P.'s at Hermits Wood.

After six months D.P. decided that Mrs Allwright must no longer soil her hands servicing half a dozen powerful motor cars, and Miss 'Truey' Clarke, a brilliant mechanic and first-rate driver, was engaged as O.C. motor cars, a job she combined with that of horse-show secretary. This meant that she was by far the hardest worked member of the establishment. From the time she was replaced by Miss Clarke, Mrs Allwright ceased to be a secretary and became D.P.'s paid companion.

It was Miss Clarke's responsibility to ensure that D.P.'s numerous cars were maintained in perfect condition, given frequent trial runs, and reported on to their owner. She accompanied D.P. and her friends on most of their outings to race meetings, horse shows, cinemas and theatres, and was sent on her own to make reports for D.P. on those occasions when she did not feel like leaving her bed – which she occupied throughout the day when she was at home. Miss Clarke worked very long hours and often when she considered that it was time to knock off she was told 'not to stir', a phrase frequently used by D.P. to her staff, as she always wanted to know exactly where everyone was. It was the long hours rather than the arduous duties which resulted in many of her secretaries leaving after comparatively short service with this eccentric millionairess.

Miss Ruth Charlton (later Mrs Charlie Smirke) was D.P.'s racing secretary who lived in London, attended race meetings with and without D.P., and telephoned Hermits Wood with the latest prices from the course when D.P. was not racing herself. Ruth was very amusing and universally popular: at D.P.'s Christmas party she gave hilariously funny sketches at D.P.'s expense which the latter loved. Once Ruth and a friend, Miss Slough, danced round the landing in a pair of D.P.'s knickers, one in each leg. One of D.P.'s most endearing qualities was that she was highly amused at jokes against herself, and she rolled about with laughter.

Francis Cassel used to refer to himself as Miss Paget's racing manager, but as Miss Charlton had been long employed as racing secretary no one knew what his exact duties were. It was perhaps not surprising that there was friction between Ruth and Sir Francis. His acquaintance with D.P. began when he returned to her some private papers she had left on a racecourse. He employed a very good-looking chauffeur called Donald, and was a little piqued when Donald married. Sir Francis had a falsetto voice and called everybody 'dear'. He lived alone in a lovely house called 'Putteridge Bury' near Luton, which is now a College of Further Education.

D.P. was an inveterate theatre-goer and was never happier than when she spent the night visiting the theatre followed by a sumptuous supper at a restaurant. Her favourite restaurants were Les Ambassadeurs, the Hungaria, the Ivy, and Prunier. On one occasion she spent six weeks at the Savoy Hotel in order, she explained, to 'do' all the theatres: she took a suite of rooms accompanied by two of her secretaries and a maid, had her meals in her private sitting room, and all her racing messages were relayed there daily from Hermits Wood.

She bothered very little about her appearance, but on the occasions on which she did decide to have her hair done she employed a Maidenhead hairdresser called Joan, who visited her on several occasions at the Savoy. Joan had to be transported by one of her secretaries, who was instructed to ask her before leaving Maidenhead whether she had a cold. I imagine Joan was particularly 'cold prone' as I have discovered six different queries as to whether she had a cold. Like so many rich eccentrics, D.P. had a horror of infection and woe betide anyone who coughed or sneezed in her presence. Joan was given dinner before embarking on her duties, which was fortunate for her, as D.P. usually waited till two or three in the morning before she allowed her to commence operations.

D.P. drank very little alcohol, her favourite drinks being Malvern water and tea. At a London restaurant, when her guests were drinking champagne, D.P. would toy with a glass of champagne and orange juice, stirring it continually with her swizzle stick, and then leave half of it. She would often horrify the head waiter at a smart restaurant by ordering endless pots of tea, and refusing to allow the old pots to be removed when a fresh pot arrived. On one occasion she had six pots on the table and the waiter had to tell her that there were no more pots available.

D.P. would always sooner create an unfavourable impression than a good one and when she arrived on a racecourse, having driven at breakneck speed, she would throw back her head and take a swig at her brandy flask. As the result of this flamboyancy it was rumoured that she was a heavy drinker, but in reality she never took more than a sip or two from her flask.

I have already referred to her superstitions: she had an aversion to green, while her favourite numbers were multiples of three, six, nine, etc., and it was ironic that she died on 9 February 1960, aged fifty-four.

D.P. had names for all her possessions. 'Hilda' was a very old and enormous Rolls-Royce, given to her by her father on her twenty-first birthday. She did not use it for many years on end, but it was taxed and insured annually 'just in case'. 'Hilda' was kept in a large shed at Pollards Wood Grange, D.P.'s second house where the majority of her secretaries had very comfortable quarters, and was given occasional airings, but never by D.P.

In her early days D.P. owned a supercharged Bugatti and a V12 Lagonda, but her favourite car in the fifties was a grey Jaguar XK120, which she called 'The Tiddler'; subsequently she changed this for an XK140. She also had a Jaguar Mark V and a Mark VII, which she called 'The Balloon'.

When D.P. visited her London dentist she took over the waiting room, which had to be laid out for an elaborate tea. Her dentist, Dr Ackner, disapproved of this, but like everyone else he was powerless in the face of D.P.'s insistence, always demanding the final appointment and becoming very put out if another patient happened to be in the waiting room on her arrival.

Charlie 'Romeo' Rogers managed her stud at Ballymacoll in Ireland, but although D.P. had spent several months each year during the war in Ireland, she never went there again after the end of the war. Olili and Mrs Allwright, however, much enjoyed their visit to Ballymacoll, a report of which follows in a subsequent chapter.

Golden Miller and Insurance were pensioned off and turned out at the Elsenham Stud in Essex where she had bred Straight Deal and which she had purchased from Sir Walter Gilbey. After Insurance died at the age of twenty-eight Golden Miller lived happily with Aggie, the Anglo-Arabian donkey of whom he became very fond.

I have already described D.P.'s disreputable old overcoat, so well known on every racecourse, which she called 'speckled hen'. Eventually some of her friends had a new coat made from the measurements of the old one, but D.P. would not wear it until she had taken it in the car to several race meetings to make sure that it did not have a curse on it. Subsequently she always referred to it as 'the coat without permission' (anything which she had not specifically ordered herself was similarly described).

D.P. loved Wimbledon and attended on as many days as possible during the fortnight. She owned several debentures and had plenty of seats at her disposal – on days she could not go herself she distributed them among her friends. When she went to the theatre, the cinema, or Wimbledon she invariably kept two seats for herself. The other seat was for 'the blue and yellow', a kind of nosebag in which she kept packets of sandwiches, bottles of aspirin and cigarettes, while

117

at race meetings the 'blue and yellow' also contained *Race-form, Chaseform* and other reference books.

Mrs Hackemer provided delicious picnic lunches for Wimbledon and D.P. declared that she was the only person who could make proper iced coffee. One secretary would be sent in advance to queue, so as to be sure of obtaining nine Wimbledon buns which D.P. and her party used to eat during the matches. D.P. also used to crack hard-boiled eggs on the back of the seat in front of her, a practice which did not endear her to its occupant.

The only occasions on which D.P. took any trouble about her appearance were on visits to the theatre. Then she would wear a silk dress together with her priceless pearls, and would smother herself in Chanel No. 5, discard her 'speckled hen' and wear a plain blue cloth coat. She smoked incessantly and carried several lighters and gold boxes which contained her cigarettes.

During the last two years of her life D.P. had dentures which she hated wearing. These were kept in a little box in the cubby hole of the car, and a secretary was ordered to remind her to put them in when she was likely to meet someone.

Unless she happened to be going to the theatre or cinema, D.P. would remain on racecourses long after the last race was run and everybody had gone home, keeping her unfortunate trainer with her discussing the horses while having a meal from a luncheon basket. Sometimes she stayed as late as 10 or 11 p.m., which did not endear her to her trainer or to the racecourse executive. On one occasion at Towcester the management declined to put the stand lights on for her, as a result of which she vowed that she would never run a horse of hers again at that meeting.

D.P.'s staff possessed considerable musical talent. In addition to Sir Francis Cassel, a concert pianist, there was Mrs Haase, a very talented operatic singer, who had performed from time to time at the Wigmore Hall under the name of Dorea Raye. Mrs Haase was a great acquisition for Miss

Paget's Christmas parties, as apart from singing she was a first-class pianist, invariably playing 'Bless this House' as D.P. descended the stairs to join the party, though D.P. had no religious beliefs. What could God do to help out if someone near her were wearing green? Mrs Haase and her husband lived at Pollards Wood Grange, and she was responsible for engaging secretaries and generally smoothing over any difficulties which might arise.

While D.P. was staying at the Savoy Olili and Mrs Allwright gave orders for the repainting of the interior of Hermits Wood, and had the much worn stair-carpet replaced. For some time the roof had leaked, but D.P. would not allow any repairs to be effected while she was in residence.

It was not meanness which caused her to allow her house to fall into a state of disrepair but 'the noise and turmoil of the workmen, and the risk of "bumping" with them'. She was not at all pleased when she returned to find these repairs had been effected 'without permission', but she soon accepted it and agreed that Olili and Mrs Allwright had done the right thing.

No member of her staff had regular hours, and when she dispensed with someone's services for that day or night it was considered very bad luck to 'bump' with her again, but as the person in question was only too anxious to go off duty this seldom occurred. She was very displeased if someone 'bumped' with her unexpectedly. Before she saw anyone it was customary for them to be sent several notes or warnings through another secretary or maid that she would be 'seen'.

Sir Francis Cassel always came to Hermits Wood on race days to receive his orders, and sometimes D.P. would send for him while she was in the loo. This would make him nervous and he would ask the maid or secretary, 'is she on the throne, dear?'

The gardeners had a difficult job to keep the grounds on the south side of the house reasonably tidy, as they were not allowed to make a noise or use the lawnmower when D.P. was asleep in the daytime. They were informed when D.P.

was likely to be out but this information had to be confirmed by a series of notes in case she changed her mind.

D.P. had Mrs Allwright's son, Alan, educated at her expense and in due course he went to Lancing College. She also promised a house to Mrs A., as she was always called, and eventually found one, though it took her a long time to make up her mind; she stayed with Mrs A. at this house for a few days shortly before her death. D.P. disliked decisions and she hated still more signing anything, but Mrs A. was a very privileged person and nothing was too good for her. Everyone supposed that D.P. would leave her and Olili the bulk of her fortune, but once again she procrastinated until it was too late.

When D.P. went racing she timed her arrival to the split second. If she had a runner in the first race she was rarely present in time to see it in the paddock – the horses would usually be at the post, and having performed with her brandy flask she would leave her car with the doors open, as near as possible to the Members' Stand, into which she would stride at the moment the starter sent the horses on their way.

Late in life, D.P. developed a craving for fish and chips, and on one occasion an unfortunate secretary had to take some congealed remains in a newspaper and show them to Mrs Hackemer (the head cook) and tell her 'this is how I want my fish cooked in future,' on Miss P.'s orders. Mrs Hackemer, who was acknowledged to be one of the finest cooks in the country, was not amused.

Although she cared nothing for her appearance she owned a few pieces of very valuable jewellery. The diamond clip she wore on her knitted beret and her pearls were worth many thousands of pounds. Day in day out, winter and summer, she wore berets which had been knitted for her by Madame Orloff. In her later years she was never seen in any other form of headgear, though previously she had worn hats with turned-up brims.

At Christmas there was always a great celebration. 'Benton's bottom' or 'Benton's foundation' (a platform) would be decorated by Miss Benton and Miss Donald. As they did not get on together the result was often incongruous – one half a summer scene with a swan and the adjoining half a winter scene with snow and Father Christmas. The house lights often fused at Christmas as a result of the number of fairy lights. The wiring was so old that one secretary told me she fully expected the house to go up in flames at any moment.

Christmas dinner was a movable feast, depending on whether D.P. was going racing at Kempton on Boxing Day. In no circumstances was a secretary allowed to go home for Christmas; D.P. would ask all of them what they would like for a Christmas gift, and the price of it depended on the length of service. It was always beautifully wrapped up by Miss Benton with very expensive ribbons and a tag 'To Miss . . . From Miss Paget'. They all had to open their presents in front of her and thank her, and were always pleased to do so as her presents were well chosen and in good taste.

D.P. was every exacting, and many of the jobs she found for her secretaries to do were unnecessary and even distasteful, but she succeeded in winning the loyalty and affection of almost every one of them.

14

'This madhouse'

The following letter from a recently-joined secretary to her mother came into my possession from an outside source:

Darling Mummy,

I am sorry not to have written before but I have been kept very busy. At the end of the day, when I am tired out, I ask myself what I have achieved, and the answer is nothing.

Miss P. makes a song and dance about everything and sometimes we have as many as seven copies of a note on the most trivial incidents. These notes have to be distributed. Everyone here, except me, and I haven't been here long enough, has a colour. No greens, of course, as Miss P. is dreadfully superstitious and won't have anything green near her. One of the girls told me that a new secretary arrived wearing green and Miss P. wouldn't even let her unpack and put her on the next train home.

I spend all my time answering the telephone, making copies of what was said, and running errands. Miss P. runs the establishment as if it were an army and she were working out a plan of campaign and wanted all ranks to know what was going on.

She sometimes sends out a note telling 'all colours' except blue that she is going to the loo. Blue is Mrs Robbins, who lives in London, and I suppose Miss P. thinks she would be finished before Mrs Robbins got the message. Miss P. is very preoccupied with the loo, and if she doesn't go she thinks she's going to die, and sends for the doctor.

Although she is so rich this is a very ordinary house and the furniture isn't nearly as nice as ours at home. We sleep at a very nice house nearby called Pollard's Wood Grange and I like it much better than Hermits Wood. This is partly because one has to go about on tiptoe here as Miss P. sleeps most of the day and raises hell if anyone wakes her up.

All the real secretarial work is done by Miss Williams, who never seems to leave Hermits Wood, and works all day and half the night. I have only spoken to her once, but she seemed very nice and helpful. Strangely enough, that goes for everyone in this madhouse, though I can't quite make out Mrs Allwright. She has a room next to Miss P.'s upstairs, while all the other secretaries either sleep downstairs or at Pollard's Wood. Although everyone likes Miss P. we are all scared stiff in case we should do something wrong, except Mrs Allwright. Mrs A., as she is always called, often goes on as if she were the boss and Miss P. her secretary. Mrs A. has a small son called Alan who is often quite cheeky, both to Miss P. and his mother, and neither of them ever ticks him off. All very odd.

Miss Olga de Mumm, who is half Russian and half German, and is called Olili, also has a room upstairs. She is a very lovely person, very quiet and serene, unlike the other members of the household. She looks very delicate. [Olili de Mumm was to die of cancer less than two years after the death of Miss Paget.]

Sir Francis Cassel lives at Luton, where I hear he has a very lovely house furnished in beautiful taste. I wonder what he thinks of Hermits Wood, with its drab walls and sticks of ugly furniture. Sir Francis seems to be Miss P.'s only man friend, and they make a strange pair. Miss P. is so masterful and domineering, while he seems so meek and mild (calling everyone 'dear' or 'darling' in a rather shrill voice. To hear them talking you'd think she was a man and he was a woman).

Although she rarely speaks to her staff except to give an order, Miss P. has a lovely speaking voice. Sir Francis calls it 'a voice of many cadences', whatever that may mean.

Miss P. orders him about and summons him to her presence, instructing him on his duties for the day in her most regal manner. I believe he makes lots of bets for her. Some of her messages to him, which are read by everyone as they go to 'all colours', are very curt, and as they say he's even richer than she is I can't understand why he stands for it. Do you think he can be a masochist? He calls himself her Racing Manager, but so does

Miss Charlton, and surely there can't be two of them. Miss C. is very nice and lots of fun, but I don't think she and Sir Francis like one another much.

I am very well and the food is lovely, but my jobs seem so pointless. I don't think Miss P. has noticed my existence, but I hear that she takes all her secretaries in turn to race meetings and horse shows, which would be great fun. She also sends them to movies, after which they have to report on the film they have seen. I should be terrified as it would be so awful if I wrote that a film was marvellous, and she went to see it on my recommendation and thought it stank. I don't know what kind of film she enjoys most, but I can't imagine it would be anything very intellectual as she only reads thrillers.

I have just heard I am to have a driving test tomorrow, and am I scared? All her cars are very powerful, quite unlike poor old Fanny [I assume this refers to her parents' car], and I don't think I shall dare change up from bottom gear. However, the secretary, Miss Clarke, who is in charge of all the cars and is an expert driver, seems a terribly nice person, and I expect she has had to try out secretaries who were just as nervous as me. Pray for me if you get this before 10.00 a.m.

Although D.P. had mellowed with the years and was, in the words of Sir Gordon Richards and 'Frenchy' Nicholson who were training for her at the time of her death, 'the perfect guvnor,' her eccentricities played a big part in her daily life as they had always done.

In the early fifties she turned against the telephone, and this new aversion threw a great deal more work on her secretaries, as every message had to be relayed and half a dozen copies made of it. There were three lines at Hermits Wood, but her trainers often found considerable difficulty in getting through to Miss Williams, who acted for Miss Paget in all her business affairs.

Charlie Rogers was very anxious that D.P. should visit the lovely Ballymacoll stud in Co. Meath, which she had bought shortly after the war and where many of the mares for which she had paid huge sums were now housed. But D.P. had become more and more disinclined to travel if it meant spending a night away from Hermits Wood, and she made a series of excuses for not going.

However, in response to Romeo's persuasion D.P. decided to send Olili and Mrs Allwright to Ballymacoll to report to her on everything they had seen. They were the two people for whom D.P. cared above all others in her life and though no two women could have been more dissimilar in character a friendship had sprung up between them. D.P. had loved Olili from long before they spent those idyllic ten months together on the banks of the Rhine in 1934–5, and until her death in 1960 no one heard a cross word pass between them.

The beautiful girl of the thirties had passed into middle age, but Olili retained all the charm and serenity which captivated everyone with whom she came in contact. 'She was a saint, always putting the wishes of others before her own,' was the opinion of one of D.P.'s secretaries. A friend who knew her well said that she invariably felt better able to cope with life after spending an hour with Olili, not so much for what Olili had said, but for the aura of well-being she radiated. But she had lost the loveliness of youth and had become so thin that when she was tired she looked almost haggard and she had a deep scar on her forehead as the result of a motor accident in Germany where she had acted as a nurse throughout the war.

Although Olili had a strong personality and was not influenced by others, she had developed some of D.P.'s peculiarities. She left herself the minimum time to reach her destination, and in consequence, like D.P., always demanded to be driven at breakneck speed. She paid only occasional visits to her lovely home in Germany, which was now occupied by her brother, as she did not get on with her sister-in-law.

Turning night into day appeared to suit D.P., but it was very hard on those whom she required to keep her company throughout the night. This night vigil was more often than not the lot of Olili and when she was seen to be losing weight it was attributed to lack of sleep, but it subsequently trans-

K*

pired that the cancer from which she died was already deep-seated.

In contrast to Olili, Barbara Allwright was an extrovert, determined to derive the maximum enjoyment from her life : she had a boisterous sense of humour and was first-rate company, though she was not universally popular with the other secretaries : those who are singled out for favouritism seldom are.

Olili, however, had become reconciled to Mrs A.'s presence at Hermits Wood, and as she loved animals and the beauties of the countryside she readily agreed when D.P. suggested that she and Mrs A. should go to Ireland to visit Rogers at Ballymacoll and make a full telephone report. They were only to be away for a few days, but although several years had passed since she had evinced much interest in the place D.P. insisted that they phone her a report at the conclusion of their inspection. One would have imagined that since Olili and Barbara A. were the only two people she really cared about D.P. would have accepted the call herself. But not a bit of it, the call had to be taken down by a secretary and relayed to D.P. with copies to all colours.

Mrs A.: We have been round Ballymacoll this afternoon and evening. It has been a perfect day and our hands are full of lovely muzzles. Alan has gone dotty about every foal, but he doesn't take any notice of an older horse unless it is a bright chestnut. It so happens that quite a few of the yearlings are chestnuts and 'Romeo' thinks they are best of the bunch. We are going to inspect the mares tomorrow. Hang on, here's Olili.

Olili: I am adoring every moment. Everyone is missing Miss Paget : she really should be here. I am sure she would enjoy it and it would be wonderful to have her with us. I think 'Romeo' was rather hurt that she did not come. We had a wonderful flight and I fell in love with Ireland at once. The horse show was super and 'Romeo' had everything laid on. He got us through all the locked doors by saying 'Miss Paget's people'. Afterwards he took us to a place called The Pocket, and all the people were so horsey they were like caricatures. After the horse show we dashed off to Phoenix Park Races where we saw the big two-year-old race, and then dashed back to the horse show where we saw Susan [Whitehead] jump twice. By this time we were terribly tired, at least I was, and I went to bed before anyone, even Alan, but as it was 12.30 it was not all that early. What a wonderful, wonderful day.

Today 'Romeo' came to lunch, and I need not tell you that it took longer than it should have done, so we were rather late starting out for Ballymacoll. 'Romeo' was in great form and carried on a running commentary about all we saw and all we were doing. He is the greatest fun. The Stud Farm is breathtakingly beautiful. First we saw a dozen mares in two paddocks, and then all the yearlings, and of course we fell in love with them all. Oh I forgot. Before doing that we inspected the house which is very comfortable. Later we saw dear wonderful Straight Deal, and it didn't seem possible that he is fifteen years old. We thought he looked much better than when we last saw him, despite the fact that this had been his busiest season for some time, and 'Romeo' told us he's served nearly forty mares. Then we went to 'Romeo's' place, and Miss Rogers gave us a wonderful tea. Barbara sat on 'Romeo's' teacup and got it all over her dress. Thank you for this wonderful trip.

Mrs A.: Would Miss Paget be interested in a nomination to Tudor Minstrel for next season? 'Romeo' says she must give a reply by tomorrow lunchtime. The man to deal with is Rex King, who used to be with M. Boussac. He told 'Romeo' he could fit him in next year but he did not mention the price. 'Romeo' thinks it would be less than Nearco. 'Romeo' is in favour of accepting the nomination though he has no particular mare in mind at the moment. Frankly, I don't believe there's all that tearing hurry, and that all Miss Paget has to do is to say she's interested. I agree with 'Romeo', Tudor Minstrel would introduce a bit of speed into our mares.

Olili: Hope ankle and tummy are better. Miss P. better start getting ready to come to Ireland for a long stay.

15

More eccentricities

Olili was paying one of her brief visits to her family in Germany when Mont Tremblant, trained by Fulke Walwyn, supplemented Golden Miller's five triumphs of 1932–6 and Roman Hackle's victory in 1940, by winning the 1952 Gold Cup. The victory of this magnificent chestnut horse brought back memories of the Miller's first success in this race, as Mont Tremblant was only a six-year-old and, like him, had been a maiden at the beginning of the season. The following letter, from a junior secretary to Olili in Germany, testifies to the affection in which this woman of Russian–German parentage was held by members of the staff at Hermits Wood.

Dear Miss de Mumm,

Yesterday was a wonderful day and we are all in the seventh heaven of delight though we all miss you and kept saying 'if only Miss de Mumm was here'. The weather at Cheltenham was filthy on all three days, and filthiest of all on the third day. Telegram was beaten in the Champion Hurdle on Tuesday, which was an awful blow, but there were genuine excuses for him as he could not act in the going. After all he was a classic horse and surely no classic race was ever run in such deep mud with the rain still teeming down.

We therefore went to Cheltenham on the Thursday in a state of alarm and despondency as it didn't seem possible that Mont Tremblant, who is only six, and the youngest horse in the field, could win as the going was worse than ever. However, I heard afterwards that Mr Walwyn never lost his confidence in our horse, and, in consequence, Miss Paget had a good bet on him at 8/1 – and as you know very few of our horses start at as long a price as that.

As always we cut it very fine, and the horses were going to post for the Gold Cup as we arrived. It was touch and go whether we should make it but we shot out of the cars and abandoned them, though the police were raising hell. I hadn't time to climb on to the stand so I watched from the lawn which was a sea of mud. I couldn't see all that well as I had to jump up and down to see over the heads of the people in front of me. When I did see, however, was Mont Tremblant racing the last fence all by himself, but he seemed to jump only half way up it and my heart stopped beating as Dave [Dick] shot up in the air. Fortunately Dave came down again on to the middle of the saddle and Mont Tremblant galloped on as if nothing had happened to win by ten lengths.

You've never seen anything like the rush of people to greet him, and how Miss Paget managed to get through the crowd to lead him in I shall never know. She must have knocked over dozens of people to get there. The excitement was terrific and I know it was a popular victory as the cheering went on and on and some of the crowd followed Mont Tremblant back all the way to the stable. Later on everyone had champagne in Miss Paget's box and I fetched Mr and Mrs Whitehead and Sue to join us. We drank your health and wished you were there.

When we got home Miss P. ordered a large meal with hot punch to be served at Pollards. She expressed instruction that it was not to be an orgy but it went on till 3 a.m. and a good time was had by all. Miss P. joined us and Ruth did one of her turns which as you know Miss P. always calls 'Ruth's nonsense'. She was very funny as always and it was a wonderful ending to a wonderful day. I am thrilled to have been present to see this triumph for Miss P. for which she waited for so many years.

I have Olili's reply from Germany written in her neat handwriting, and I know that the recipient regards it as one of her most treasured possessions.

Dear Miss ——,
Many a time did I want to thank you for every one of your

delightful 'reports'. Couldn't find the proper words, and so, oh shame, no words whatsoever of thanks have reached you yet. Need I tell you how much I appreciated your various reports. Please don't take it too badly that I only today say: 'Very, very many thanks'. Am spending eight days in Ansbach for the beloved Bach festival, hearing heavenly music, morning and night (unfortunately not at noon). It's quite wonderful to be here, but it will also be wonderful to be with you all again at Hermits Wood. Many a comment could I make on all the happenings at Hermits Wood which you described so delightfully, but shall leave my comments till we met again. Please remember me to everyone at Hermits Wood. Again my thanks.

Yours sincerely, Olili de Mumm.

The recipient has described to me how all those who had been in D.P.'s employ for any length of time loved her.

[D.P.] was a most exacting employer and worked us extremely hard, but had anyone spoken disparagingly of her in our presence we would have scratched their eyes out.

Olili, however, inspired a different kind of love, which almost amounted to reverence. She was such an instinctively good person that one knew it would be quite impossible for her to be unkind or unselfish, though she had a very strong personality. Yes, we all loved Miss P. for the qualities she tried so hard to hide from us, but I, for one would have laid down my life for Olili.

As I have already stated only a fraction of the correspondence which was found stacked in piles reaching to the ceiling after Miss Paget's death has reached me, but I think it is sufficient to allow my readers to imagine D.P.'s life-style at Hermits Wood and her obsession with detail. The following is a letter written in her own hand and presumably dictated over the telephone to her medical adviser.

Dr Phillips:

It is most disturbing, this apparent illness of one of my secretaries, as at the moment we are short-handed as Miss Williams is away on a holiday. Anyway please report officially and in detail what is the matter with her. Is it definitely flu, and might it not be the possible beginning of a spotty disease? How high is her temperature? Exactly what have you told her to do? What medicines have you prescribed and can she be on duty tomorrow, Friday, or when?

Naturally, I don't want any risk of these germs spreading so if there is any risk of infection is not it better that she remains in isolation in her chalet? But I must, repeat, must know how long it may take, and when I know I might get someone in to help. I want you to use this chance to really *frighten* her about her size. Everyone has tried here, but she does not seem to care, which is fantastic at her age. I have had a nurse in the house who gave her intelligent talks, but she pays no heed to anyone, and I know her parents are also worried. She might listen to a doctor, and you can say that being that size and being an *enormous* eater she is much more likely to pick up germs. Anyway, frighten her about this because it is only for her own good and report to me at once when you have done this.

I would like you to give me some vitamin pills. I am very well, except that out of the blue I am pretty constipated, a thing which I have never been in all my life, and I think it is because I don't get good green vegetables. So what pills could substitute for that? You had better send me a bottle. If she mentions that Miss Williams and Miss Paget are overweight you must say that as we are made of sterner stuff it does not apply to us. You can also add that Mrs Haase is enormous, and she is always ill. What do you suggest for my constipation?

Dr Phillips replied as follows:

No, it is not a spotty disease, you can call it 'summer flu'. It usually takes three days. There is an epidemic of it going round, and I have treated several cases of it. She will not be fit before Monday at the very earliest, her temperature is 100° this morning but that is not really a guide and it may go up again this evening, and it will take several days before it returns to normal, night and morning. She is a nice child, and is making very light of it. There is no treatment which will make any difference, and it is bound to run its course. I have prescribed aspirins and fluids. She will definitely not be fit to resume work on Friday. There is a risk of infection – very much so. She should remain in her chalet at least till over the weekend. I will come and see her again tomorrow. I have made a note of all Miss Paget says. I will bear

131

it in mind and speak to her in due course. She is a little too ill at the moment for me to give her a pep talk on diet. As far as possible people should keep away from her except those directly concerned with her meals.

For Miss Paget, I would suggest vitamin C to compensate for the lack of green vegetables, but if the constipation requires more than just vitamin C pills I suggest there should be a complete reassessment of her diet. I will give a prescription at the chemist which should be ready at 12.30. Please give Miss Paget my very kind regards.

The Wimbledon Fortnight was one of the highlights in D.P.'s life, and the following notes in her handwriting give some idea of the organization which preceded her advance on the Centre Court. She was often referred to by her junior secretaries as 'the General', and no military commander could have planned his undertaking with more meticulous care in order to ensure that nothing went wrong on the big day.

Wimbledon General Orders
Staff breakfast 8.00 a.m.
Dining room breakfast 8.30 a.m.
All food ready, including tea, cakes by 11.30 a.m., also sandwiches for Miss Clarke [secretary responsible for all transport].
Five-seater Jaguar and Lagonda at front door at 11.00 a.m.
Note to Miss Clarke, very important.
Definitely tune radios both cars on to the Home Service without any possible mistake before we go. Also, have right hand window of the Tiddler [the car she would drive herself] open.
You must learn by heart every item packed in five-seater.
I am much fussier at Wimbledon with my luggage than I am at a race meeting.
Go now, and when you arrive Wimbledon park your car clearly.
Vamp all police on duty.* There must be no hitch of any sort.
Meet me at 1.45, where I unload, having with you loo ladies, programmes, and loo ladies' cushions. Also their buns etc. Have these on your arm and DO NOT STIR. Teacase remains Lagonda. Other Lagonda luggage store in loo, including food cases.

* The Oxford Dictionary defines the verb 'to vamp' as 'to set to work on a man to attract him sexually'. I doubt whether this was Miss Paget's precise meaning.

Day No. 2 Orders
All cars tuned to Home Service.
Nearly certain Miss Paget drives five-seater today so PUT SEAT
TO MY DISTANCE. [In written messages D.P. nearly always
refers to herself as Miss Paget though she occasionally employs
first person.]
The following items you put in the loo on arrival, speckled hen
[her overcoat], lambs loo [I do not know what this refers to], the
blue and the straw [two bags].
Food cases also go in loo as yesterday. Authorities accuse loo
ladies of pocketing my money paid them for cushions. Investigate
and report. Insist, however, it is no business of mine.

Miss Paget's trainers were instructed to run as few of her
horses as possible during Wimbledon, when she never went
racing herself – she was furious if anything cropped up to
prevent her watching the tennis, and even 'Romeo' was not
welcome, as the following undated memo affirms:

After you have got the order of play tonight on Centre Court
and No. 1 Court, read the Centre Court Play to Mrs Robbins then
tell her if no change by 12 o'clock tomorrow, you, Mrs Robbins
go straight to Wimbledon Centre Court sit in your seats, don't
stir, wait for Miss Paget's arrival. 'Romeo' being here has ruined
Wimbledon and I have again been beaten in a photo finish, my
third in a week. Have repeatedly told trainers disastrous to run
horses during Wimbledon. Will they never learn?

Although D.P. had a pathological hatred of journalists she
was a most prolific purchaser of newspapers; but it would
be incorrect to describe her as an avid reader. Having scanned
the racing column and the few paragraphs devoted to show
jumping, she would throw the paper on the floor and summon
one of her staff to come and fold it up. Anyone suspected of
throwing away a newspaper without D.P.'s permission was
in disgrace.

At Hermits Wood there were rooms and sheds for the
storage of D.P.'s junk, but her insistence on keeping all newspapers for a period of at least three months presented a
serious problem when she spent that month at the Savoy

Hotel 'doing' the theatres. At the end of a week her suite had become uncomfortably full even for D.P., accustomed as she was to having newspapers strewn over every room, so she instructed her maid to make a pile of them and place them in the corridor outside her door, with a notice attached in capital letters, 'NOT TO BE TOUCHED OR MOVED UNDER ANY CIRCUMSTANCE'. This resulted in a visit from the management, who explained that she was not only contravening the rules of the hotel, but also an LCC by-law which forbade the deposit of any article in the corridor of an hotel.

In the next few days the ever-increasing pile of newspapers alternated between D.P.'s suite and the corridor, but eventually she had to submit and say 'You win.' She had behaved more unreasonably than usual. By the time her stay was up there were piles of newspapers and periodicals several feet high in her suite, and a special car was sent to transport them to Hermits Wood, though it was odds of 100–1 against her looking at any of them again.

As D.P. only read the sports pages she knew little or nothing about politics, but this did not prevent her referring to herself as an ardent Conservative. When asked why she replied, 'because I dislike being ruled by the lower classes.' On polling day she would order her car five minutes before the poll closed to take her to the polling station two miles away. In the same way that she insisted that her dentist should give her his last appointment she wanted to be the last to cast her vote, taking with her her own pencil, 'in case the horrible socialists should have stolen the public pencils.'

On one occasion she arrived as the hand of the clock was approaching zero hour and made two crosses against the Tory member's name. Mrs A., who had accompanied her to the polling station, pointed out that this might invalidate her vote, so she was given another paper. As she left a weary official remarked, 'thank God there's only one Dorothy Paget.'

In the middle fifties Mr Fred Neilson, the distinguished throat and nose specialist, received a call from D.P.'s doctor, informing him that D.P. had a swelling in her throat and was convinced she had glandular fever. Would Mr Neilson ring up Miss Paget at Hermits Wood and arrange an appointment for her? This Mr Neilson did, suggesting that D.P. should visit him in Harley Street: he received a reply from a secretary that Miss Paget would do nothing of the sort, but that Mr Neilson should visit her at Hermits Wood as soon as possible.

On his arrival, Mr Neilson found D.P. in excellent health but suffering discomfort from a small stone in the gland which secretes saliva. He considered that it should be removed and suggested that she come to the London Clinic the following week, assuring her that it would require only a minor operation and that she would be able to go home the next day. D.P. replied that nothing would induce her to go to London and insisted that the operation should be performed in a small nursing home only a few miles from her home on the outskirts of High Wycombe. Mr Neilson asked her to arrive a couple of hours before the operation but, running true to form, D.P. turned up with only twenty minutes to spare. She was given a sedative and placed on a canvas stretcher, but the canvas was not up to her weight and she crashed to the floor, all twenty-odd stone of her. Mr Neilson told me that he was already in the theatre and did not witness the accident, but he heard the crash and the sound of a very angry female voice.

A stouter stretcher was found, and D.P. was taken back to her room, where enough dope was administered to her to stop three hot favourites. She appeared to be asleep when she was finally deposited in the theatre, but as she was being placed on the operating table she was obviously very wide awake, and sitting bolt upright demanded, 'Is this an operating theatre, it looks like a kitchen to me! Mr Neilson, I hope you are concentrating, and I also hope that neither you nor any of your assistants has a cold.' The operation was entirely successful and D.P. returned home the following day in the best of health except for a few bruises.

Several months later Fred Neilson was watching tennis on the Centre Court at Wimbledon and saw D.P. sitting two rows in front of him. In the course of the afternoon she turned round and, recognizing him, said, 'Mr Neilson, how very fortunate, you are just the man I want to see. I have a slightly sore throat and would like you to examine it.' With that she faced him and opening her mouth as wide as it would go exclaimed 'Ah.' Those sitting in the row between D.P. and Mr Neilson who had paid good money to watch tennis on a smooth green court, found themselves looking down a vast red tunnel. Mr Neilson explained that the Hippocratic oath did not permit him to carry out his professional duties on the Centre Court, but said that he would send her some lozenges.

On wonders how D.P., with her terror for infection, would have reacted had she found herself in the position of the unfortunate people sitting in the row between herself and Mr Neilson.

16

'I am desperately fussy'

Visits to the theatre and restaurants were also preceded by orders of the day to her staff, and the following plan of campaign was a typical specimen.

To Mrs Haase:
Go to London, do blues [reports on all messages for Mrs Robbins], Calendar [fetch racing Calendar], and also lodge Weatherby's Miss Clarke's 'authority to act'.
Theatre seats for Saturday, last house, struggle like hell, you must get me something somewhere, minimum four seats, two and two if you can't do better, maximum six seats.
First choice, Separate Tables. Second choice, Serious Charge. Third choice, Uncertain Joy, find out if Ursula Jeans will be performing. Also report immediately how you think I would react to Maurice Chevalier. Has he a chorus with him? Report from London what the situation is and when you bring Calendar don't stir as I might see you. In any case report Miss Clarke 2 p.m. Make a note of conjuror called Fred Caps (Kaps? Karf?) in Magic Circle programme TV last night. He would be first class for a party. David Nixon's secretary might help in this.

Two days later:

To Mrs Haase:
Please reserve me tonight a table for 6 for Quaglinos, the basement part of their establishment. I must have the same table as last time – sofa table bang opposite the stage. You must talk to the Head Manager and confirm all this with him again at 5 p.m.

as I am desperately fussy and insist I am looked after properly. I think I will sell two seats and stick to the four seats for Garrick Theatre tonight. Report back about all this.

On another occasion on which D.P. was on a jaunt to London the following instructions were handed to a secretary:

At 2.15 precisely telephone the Ambassadeurs and talk to the correct manager or Julian the head waiter. Reserve a table for 4 for Miss Paget tomorrow Saturday night after the theatre. She must, repeat must, have a corner table, and will not, repeat not, sit on top of the band, which was where she was made to sit last time and was deafened by noise. Also warn head waiter Julian to be on the look out for Miss Paget's arrival and to put an un-iced bottle of Malvern water on table.

Prior to a further visit to the theatre D.P. sent this message to her cook Mrs Hackemer:

A tender Irish Stew in two dishes with nine pieces of meat ready so that I can eat at any time after 4.30 p.m. Iced coffee must be ready 5.30 p.m. also theatre sandwiches made up sardines, chicken and ham, with lettuce. Very important about lettuce. [One assumes she was no going on to a supper party at a restaurant that evening.] Return all your orders tonight, also elaborate food list week-end. Expect especially good hot dinner Sunday night.

The only member of Miss Paget's entourage who did very much as she pleased was Mrs Allwright, who was not even a senior secretary, while Sir Francis Cassel, who was, of course, never in her employ, had to mind his Ps and Qs (one of D.P.'s favourite expressions). She enjoyed his company, and when he was in favour she almost invariably took him racing with her and sent him to represent her when she was not present. But, in her own words, 'I don't let him take any liberties' – I hasten to add that these did not refer to her person, but that she would not stand for his meddling in matters which were none of his business.

Her association with the Nicholson family was a particularly happy one, and D.P. trusted Mrs Nicholson's judgement not only about the horses her husband trained but also the men who rode them. Mrs Nicholson was well informed too, concerning horses trained in other stables which Miss Paget's horses might be called upon to meet in the near future and it was she who dealt with the voluminous correspondence which training a string of horses for D.P. inevitably entailed, thereby allowing her husband to get on with the business of training them.

The following is a message from D.P., presumably phoned by one of her secretaries to Mrs Nicholson. The message is marked 'Private, not for distribution, copies to Miss de Mumm and Mrs Allwright only':

Do you find D. Dick [her jockey] in any way unsatisfactory? I am not fond of Sir Francis Cassel's mentality as you may have gathered from several of my messages to you, and it is why I have not sent him steeplechasing much this season. Out of the blue again he has once more produced a strong 'anti' D. Dick. Do you know anything about this or why? I am quite willing to believe that the Epsom people got together and had a banco on Mr Wiggs. But if they did this and burnt their fingers it was their own silly fault, and no concern of mine. I had foreseen this arising and it is why in a previous message I *advised against* employing G. as I knew from experience he was in up to his neck with the Epsom people. Anyway I do *not* consider this my business, and I am more than satisfied with D. Dick. However, I want to check up with you.

Cassel laps up D. Dick's gossip. I never do, because I know Dick too well. Anyway, if Cassel telephones with any silly tales don't let them worry you. I was not born yesterday, and am well able to look after my own affairs. But I just wanted to check with you before Cassel's snowball became a snowman.

Naturally, D. Dick looked ill yesterday, because he hadn't eaten for 36 hours though Cassel implied it was because he had lost a packet on Mr Wiggs. His Epsom friends may have lost their shirts on him, but that is no concern of mine and as long as owner, trainer and jockey trust one another everything should be a success. Cassel is *not* to undermine this.

139

Mrs Nicholson's reply to D.P.'s message was as follows:

No, I do not find D. Dick unsatisfactory, though yesterday I think he rode a bad race, but all jockeys do that occasionally. The reason for it was I think that he had a bee in his bonnet about a horse called Mercator and thought it was a good thing, and that it had been 'very strong' at the last meeting. In actual fact it had been trying for its life and is just a moderate horse. Dave lost his head and went chasing after Mercator in the early part of the race and never gave his horse a chance. Rest assured, however, he's all right. I understand it is a private message for you only and Miss de Mumm and Mrs Allwright, and I understand how you feel about Sir Francis. D. Dick needs a firm hand and is inclined to do silly things, but there is no harm in him and we both like him and consider him not only just a first class jockey, but the best. So long as he is given to understand that you won't stand for any monkey business everything will be fine. I am sure we couldn't find a better jockey, and he is the best steeplechase rider we have seen for a long time. He tries very hard and his only fault is that is inclined to go to the front too early.

I don't think 'Frenchy' minds people backing our horses when they win, but he would be rather concerned if the wrong people got to know when one is not much fancied. There are as you know people around who would try and get a jockey to drop one out which was very short [a hot favourite]. I am certain that neither Dave nor any other jockey who rides for us would do it off his own bat, but it must be impressed on them that Miss Paget is very much against her hot favourites getting beaten, and it creates a bad impression if her jockeys mix with the wrong sort of people.

Dave was a bit downhearted after Mr Wiggs had been beaten. I think all his pals were on it, as were all our stable lads. Everyone seemed to think 'this one *will* win'. It's no use, they will never learn.

In contrast to the two previous messages between D.P. and Mrs Nicholson the following message from D.P. to Sir Francis Cassel went to 'all colours':

Francis, you cannot go yet, but tell Mrs Paul and Miss Clarke to meet me at 1.50 for the first race, also you and Miss Griffie if she goes early, but she must go early. You must meet 'Romeo' and get the latest dope about Amstel, and if he really thinks the filly might win, and if it is worth my having something on her. At the moment I have no bet on the 2 o'clock race. Also I want you to phone the draw in case I am still here. Get me nine race cards and order me two tables directly after the 4 o'clock race.

I have described how D.P. would go to infinite trouble to assure that everything went according to plan on a big occasion, but the following will illustrate that her attendance at an unimportant jumping meeting at Windsor was preceded by an order of the day leaving nothing to chance:

Message to Secretary:
Herewith two badges, No. 14 you, No. 17 Mrs Coope. Three car park badges, No. 7 the car I go in, No. 33 the car you drive, No. 34 Sir Francis.
New Mark VII front door 10.30 a.m., also Rover. Tiddler warmed up because I might change my mind and drive Tiddler. If no change you go in Rover, plus Mrs Coope, and us in new Mark VII. Midday papers, you better get so you ought to leave not moment later than 11.30 you meet me 12.40 with nine race cards and three pairs race glasses on your shoulder. Show Mrs Coope the loo, eating places and everything. Both of you have blocks, pencils etc.
You pick me up again directly after first race. Will probably want tea directly after 2 o'clock race. Warn them to keep food in the place we were in after The Saint won. Warn the loo lady I am coming, also the police. Both of you get copies of the times of Granada Cinema. If I go to a movie one of you will have to collect Betty, evening paper etc. Hold your thumbs for Straight Lad.

In the fifties show-jumping played a big part in D.P.'s life for which she owned a number of very successful horses trained for her by Mr and Mrs Whitehead. Mrs Whitehead was a fine rider and had a wonderful way with horses, which were ridden in the show ring by her attractive daughter Sue, who started reeling off clear rounds when barely nineteen.

Although everyone remembers Colonel Harry Llewellyn and Foxhunter as they were the founders of what, largely thanks to television, has become a major international sport, triumphs in the show-jumping ring are ephemeral and the heroes of yesterday soon forgotten. I will therefore not attempt to describe the numerous horses which represented D.P. successfully in dozens of shows all over the country and at Harringay and the White City, though I must mention Scorchin, who was one of the most successful and popular jumpers in the country for a number of years. Later he was trained by Pat Smythe, who rode him with outstanding success in a number of events.

Although she was one of the world's greatest spenders and would give a blank cheque to her agent for some yearling she had never seen, D.P. could strike a very hard bargain, and when she sold some animal, having assured herself that it was past its best, she would haggle over a matter of guineas and pounds. Before the introduction of decimal currency, horses sold at public auction were paid for in guineas, the odd shillings going to the auctioneers, but private sales were conducted in pounds. D.P. had a long harangue and endless correspondence with some Japanese buyers who eventually bought her horse Eforegiot. She asked the Japanese three thousand for him, not stating whether they were guineas or pounds, but they beat her down and she eventually agreed to two thousand five hundred. She had stuck out for two thousand seven hundred for over a week, but when she realized that she had met her match in the men from the Orient she eventually gave way. To add insult to injury she was paid in pounds, at which she protested strongly, but with no success. After the sales were over, D.P. sent the following message to the Bloodstock Agency which had acted for her:

Please officially write at once Eforegiot is now the property of your firm, and no more Miss Paget's responsibility. Miss Paget is heartbroken that she has sold him, it is like being disloyal to an old friend so she would particularly like to know what happens to him from now onwards and wishes them luck with him etc. The horse is NOT insured, but take note I am NOT, repeat NOT, responsible for him any more.

It was of course, sheer hypocrisy to pretend to be heart-broken. After all, she was selling him for a trifling sum equivalent to the kind of saving bet she might make on the horse she felt likely to defeat the one on which she'd had a banco.

D.P. learned early in her career as an owner of racehorses that what the Jockey Club and the National Hunt Committee said was law and that there was nothing she could do about it. Had she won the Gimcrack Stakes she would undoubtedly have told both bodies what she thought of them in her speech as guest of honour, but apart from getting a number of grievances off her chest her condemnation would have been to no avail.

Show-jumping, however, was a comparatively recent innovation and she fully expected that so liberal a patron as herself would automatically be granted special privileges. But the Show Jumping Association, although welcoming the patronage of Britain's wealthiest spinster, made it perfectly clear that she would have to accept the rulings of the committee just like everyone else. The following message was dispatched to the Show Jumping Association and 'to whom it may concern' at Harringay:

Harringay and Time Schedule:
Miss Paget wrote Colonel [now Sir Mike] Ansell a very important letter which she can only believe must have gone astray, particularly asking that Scorchin should be permitted to jump in Section 3 of class 9, which is jumped Thursday night. This would mean Miss Paget and all her friends would see him jump for dead certain. To Miss Paget's horror she has just studied the draw and sees that Scorchin is drawn in the Second Section, which is jumped Thursday morning. So will you please approach Colonel Ansell personally to get permission for Scorchin to jump on Thursday night so Miss Paget and party could see him. Also

143

please inform me if he is drawn in the Third Section in the Daily Telegraph Cup which is jumped on Friday evening. If he is not jumped in the Third Section again Miss Paget would not see him. Miss Clarke and Blackmore must telephone Colonel Ansell or his private secretary or Captain Webber as by hook or by crook Scorchin must jump in Class 9 Thursday night. This had been done before and everyone must realize how desperately important this is to Miss Paget so fight like bloody hell as it will bitch all her plans for the whole week if she does not hear something definite today. Copies to all colours.

17

'Instantly type me an endlessly long report'

The majority of people considered that D.P.'s interest in show-jumping would be short-lived, as she generally viewed horses as animals for which you paid large sums hoping they would win races, preferably classic races, the Grand National or the Gold Cup at Cheltenham. And whether or not they rose to these heights there was a reasonable chance they might land a banco for her from time to time. No one therefore believed that she would keep horses for any length of time whose sole objective was a sequence of clear rounds.

But they were wrong. D.P. got bitten by the show-jumping bug, and after one of her horses had won a big event she told her show-jumping secretary that when a horse of hers was still clear with only two more fences to jump she derived a thrill comparabe to that when a horse on which she had a banco had its head in front with only a few strides to go.

Training for D.P. was a mixed blessing as far as Mrs Whitehead was concerned. An empathy existed between herself and her horses, and she was never so happy as when she was engaged in training them and looking after their welfare in her stables but the paperwork entailed in training horses for D.P., whether on the flat, under N.H. rules or for show-jumping, drove Mrs Whitehead nearly mad.

Men and women who had been decorated for bravery and

those who were fearless riders to hounds would quail at the approach of D.P., and Mrs Whitehead freely admitted that she scared the living daylights out of her. When D.P. signalled her to her side at a show and led off with, 'Mrs Whitehead, you have not replied to my memoranda, will you kindly tell me . . .' a series of questions would follow: whether so-and-so having been entered here, should be jumped here or there; which competition would take least winning; who would ride so-and-so, and could they not get so-and-so to ride such-and-such? What time was his class? Had he a good chance? Should she be there to see him?

Coherent thought is apt to evaporate as the result of a bombardment such as this, and on one occasion poor Mrs Whitehead took to her heels, ostensibly to fetch her entry books but primarily to escape from the barrage which, in her own words, turned her into a gibbering idiot.

The widespread misapprehension that D.P. was devoted to animals was the result of stories which appeared from time to time in the Press – whenever an editor found himself short of copy for a feature article he would summon one of the females sitting around the office and instruct her to do a human interest story on the Hon. Dorothy Wyndham Paget. I need hardly add that the unfortunate woman could never get within a mile of her, and sooner than return to the office empty-handed she would fall back on her imagination, a quality which every feature writer worthy of the name possesses in abundance.

One enterprising woman described how the Hon. Dorothy Wyndham Paget was never so happy as when she was in the stable cuddling her horses. D.P. was one of the least cuddly women who ever lived. The feature writer was only being logical when she imagined that D.P. was devoted to horses since why otherwise did she keep about four hundred? Logic, however, was of little assistance when assessing the likes, dislikes and habits of D.P., who, in fact, regarded her horses in the same way as a gambler at a casino regards his pile of chips – something with which you can have a great deal of fun, and, if you're lucky, win a great deal of money.

One of D.P.'s shortcomings was that she was reluctant to offer a horse for sale until it had proved conclusively that it was no longer any good. Occasionally she would enter horses which were likely to win in their class at a sale, but more often than not would withdraw them at the last moment. The only occasion on which an autioneer could be sure of spirited bidding for one of D.P.'s horses was after it had won a selling race, as nine times out of ten the horse was much better than the average selling plater and D.P. had landed a banco over it. She was very naive on some matters, and she never learnt that in order to sell her trash she must from time to time sell a horse which would pay its way, and perhaps even prove a bargain.

It was a positive illness to her when some horse she had sold won a race. When in due course she had so many horses that not even she could find races for them all and she put several good-class horses up for auction, bidders smelt a rat, or thought they did, and the horses were knocked down for a quarter of their true value. In 1948 she sent Fine Prospect, one of the best handicappers in this country to the Newmarket sales hoping to get 10,000 guineas for him. But he was sold to her great friend Charlie 'Romeo' Rogers for 2,500 guineas, easily the biggest bargain this shrewd trainer ever picked up in his long and successful career! A little later that year a batch of thirteen horses of all ages fetched 3,500 guineas.

If any man could influence her it was 'Romeo' Rogers but not even he, using all his charm, could induce her to come over to Ireland and visit her stud at Ballymacoll. Sir Gordon Richards, who had a great affection for her, and would never hear a word said against her, admitted to me that in the five years she trained with him she never once visited his stables, and he was not at all sure that she even knew where they were. Nor did she ever speak to him on the telephone, for all such business as entries, forfeits, acceptances and scratchings was channelled through Miss Williams.

A typical example of the kind of horse that D.P. was pre-

147

pared to sell was Prestbury, who had been a pretty useful animal in his day but had failed to contribute towards his keep for over a year as the result of infirmities. She therefore sent the following message to her trainer. 'There is a little man who bought two horses off me, and, believe it or not, I hear he might buy another. Should I offer him Prestbury, or is he noticeably lame?' Her trainer answered :

Yes, I suppose you could offer him as I think he might get sound again if he was rested, though it is impossible to put a price on him. He has a curby hock, and he has been fired in front, but I don't think it shows. On the other hand he makes a hell of a noise [he had gone in his wind], which everyone must realize who has heard him gallop. He has an awful mouth – he opens it wide and sticks his head one way and goes the other. He is quiet enough, but I am afraid there is no chance of his making a show horse. He is still lame, but only from the curb which is not all that serious.

Robert was D.P.'s elderly parrot; no one ever knows the age of a parrot, but D.P. had had him a long time and she said he was no chicken when he came into her possession. He lived in the servants' hall, so she seldom saw him, but although quite a lot of his feathers were of the forbidden colour green, she regarded Robert as a mascot. Her superstitions themselves were subject to revision and often what had been considered propitious on Monday had assumed the evil eye by the end of the week. Robert, however, had never been suspected of contributing to the lack of success of any of her horses. On one of the rare occasions on which she entered the servants' quarters to converse with him she found that he was far from his usual sunny self and in a memo to a secretary she wrote 'Robert is bloody ill, fetch a vet at once, understand best is at Whipsnade. Tell him Robert's condition is serious and highly suspicious. If worst happens he must perform autopsy. Require detailed report soonest.'

Doping, or nobbling as it was called, became a universal topic of conversation as the result of tests on horses which had run unaccountably badly which revealed that a narcotic had been administered. It was suspected that one of the methods employed was to spray a horse while it was being led around the paddock prior to a race. To counteract this D.P. designed a fetlock-length sheet which enveloped the horse from the tip of its ears all the way to its hoofs – a very sensible precaution. Possibly as a result of it there is no record of a horse of D.P.'s having been found to be doped – though a number of them indeed ran inexplicably poorly, at any rate as far as D.P. was concerned.

From the above memo it is evident that D.P. suspected that Robert had been nobbled, though since no stranger was ever permitted to enter the portal of Hermits Wood she must have thought it was an inside job. The following reply from the secretary the next day must have allayed her suspicions:

I drove to Dunstable to fetch the head Whipsnade Zoo vet, Mr Martin Senior. He struck me as extremely efficient, in fact I think he is easily the best vet who has come into this house. He is responsible for all the animals and birds at Whipsnade and I am afraid it was obvious as soon as Mr Senior saw Robert that he did not think much of his chances, and that it is only a matter of time, unless a miracle happens. However Mr Senior has done his best. He examined Robert carefully, gave him a drop of brandy and water and a pill of some kind. Robert's heart is in a very bad state, in fact it has collapsed, probably as a result of the bad condition of his liver and a growth on his lung. He has lost weight and his breast bone is like a razor. Mr Senior will come again tomorrow. He does not suspect foul play so if the worst happens will you still require autopsy?

When the worst did happen a few days later, D.P. accepted the veterinary surgeon's verdict of death from natural causes.

D.P. owned several dogs, but the only one definitely named in the records in my possession is Sabu. In a memo to a secretary D.P. wrote, 'Sabu has taken to lifting his leg in the house. This is absurd at his age, and must be stopped forthwith.' I suspect the recipient was Mrs Allwright, as no one else would have dared give the following reply. 'You are asking quite a lot. Have you ever tried to stop a dog lifting

149

his leg? Sabu is no different from other dogs and does not ring me up and tell me when he is going to do it.'

A few weeks later there was more correspondence about a bad leg. It does not state whether it was his 'lifting' leg or how he came to hurt it, but D.P. reported 'Sabu's leg in filthy condition, inform vet. Miss Mumm bandaged it correctly. If too tight he will chew his leg off.'

Junior secretaries came and went, but the arrival of a new one invariably entailed a vast amount of correspondence to every member of the staff, who had to help instruct the newcomer in every detail of her duties until she had the routine off by heart. Although nine-tenths of this routine was superfluous it nevertheless had to be learned. The only job of real importance was that of testing the newcomer's competence not only to drive the numerous makes of cars in her employer's possession but to drive them at high speed, as nine times out of ten they would be striving to make a deadline, and woe betide them if they failed.

D.P. invariably drove herself, at any rate on the outward journey, until the last years of her life. Having learned to drive racing cars at Brooklands in her youth she was a magnificent driver and drove at furious speeds. Only once, however, have I found that she fell foul of the law and was summoned for dangerous driving. A police driver gave evidence that he chased a car to Kempton Park races and he thought from the speed at which it was driven it had been stolen. But the driver was Miss Dorothy Paget, racehorse owner, the police officer told the magistrates at Feltham Police Court. In a sixty mph chase Miss Paget was alleged to have driven across red traffic lights, causing another car to swerve and brake violently, overtaken a second car, and forced three cyclists on to the kerb. Next, her car took bends 'in as nearly a straight line as possible', and cleared a humpbacked bridge at fifty mph.

When her name was called there was no response, and her counsel Mr Edgedale told the chairman, 'Miss Paget is here but is too frightened to appear.' But as the chairman was not standing for that, D.P. was eventually coaxed into court, where she told the magistrates, 'I was in a hurry to get to Kempton, but when I got there my horse was beaten by a short head. It was not my lucky day.' D.P. was fined £10 for driving dangerously and £25 for ignoring the traffic lights.

Driving tests for new secretaries were the job of Miss Clarke, and the following instructions coincided with the arrival of a Mrs Hancock and a Miss Puckering:

From Miss Paget:

The newcomers will probably appear about 12 o'clock and the sooner you start on your car tests the better. Take both of them to save time, and they must each have their blocks with them on which to make notes of places etc. Start off with the Rover as she is the most normal car, but not for long as Judy [another secretary] will need her to take Mrs Robbins to the station. Then Blue Baby. Then I insist, yes I insist (unless they are both bad drivers), you take them out in one of the big cars. It anyway would do The Balloon (Mark VII) a helluva lot of good to have a run, and if the roads aren't too bad they ought to handle the 3.4. Even if they are, you could show them all the knobs. Show them all places of interest, garages etc. also the car books. Naturally show them Rufus's sleeping quarters as apparently he was very funny with them last night. [As D.P. had no male employees I imagine Rufus was another dog.] Spend hours with them, and they have been told you are going to give an honest report so they won't try any funny business. I will be disappointed if report is bad, but I must know the truth. I would love to know their reaction. Instantly type me an endlessly long report, what sort of women are they, how they drive, and how you like each and why, and exactly what you did with them today. Send this all colours, and give blue envelope to Miss Williams to send Mrs Robbins in London with other blues.

Apparently the initial tests satisfied D.P., as a few days later, following Miss Clarke's report, she wrote a further note 'Take both women out in Mark VII and make them drive it faster.' And finally this note was despatched: 'Instruct new women take things easily this afternoon as they will be seen tonight. Instruct them keep quiet while under here.' Which, being interpreted, meant that she was going to interview them, and that they must not disturb D.P.'s sleep while they were in the secretaries' room, which was below her bedroom. It was the last message despatched by D.P. to the secretary in charge of her fleet of cars. Ten days later she died.

18

D.P.'s last ride

D.P.'s life cannot be judged by the standards we apply to the lives of other people. The widespread belief that she was lonely and discontented was untrue, and from the time she took up residence at Hermits Wood, when she was still in her mid-thirties, she would not have changed places with any woman living. As the result of her hostility to the outside world she eliminated many possible sources of enjoyment, but that was the way she wanted it. She revelled in her dictatorship, which gave her a feeling of self-importance and suppressed the inferiority complex which had marred her early life.

Largely through her own fault she did not enjoy success on the turf commensurate with her colossal outlay, but she won seven Cheltenham Gold Cups, a record which may stand for all time, and both the Grand National and the Derby, a feat only once previously accomplished, and that by a man who a year later became King of England. She landed some gigantic bets, which were ever fresh in her mind, while the even bigger ones she lost were forgotten within a few minutes of her secretary, Miss Williams, despatching cheques to her bookmakers.

The two people she loved lived with her, and in Miss Williams, Miss Charlton (Mrs Smirke) and Miss Clarke she had three secretaries she could trust with her life. Her scope for happiness was admittedly limited but the belief that selfishness invariably breeds discontent did not apply to her. D.P. lived in the grand manner and found it most agreeable. She was not an imaginative woman, and as the physical proximity of men was so distasteful she could not miss what she had never wanted.

D.P. died as she would have wished to die, planning the future of her horses, with no fuss and no outside interference from newspaper reporters demanding bulletins on her health. Turning night into day the only fresh air she inhaled was when she went racing, which, combined with upwards of a hundred cigarettes a day and an ever-increasing intake of food, was not conducive to longevity.

Throughout her life she repeatedly sent out messages to 'all colours' that she was not well, and nine times out of ten these messages were followed within the hour by an order to the cook on duty to send up a large meal. In the last year her messages complaining of her health had become more frequent, as had the demands for larger and larger meals. It has been suggested that her craving for food was the result of a serious complaint, but this was not supported by the medical evidence which stated that her death was due to heart failure accentuated by the fact that she was very much overweight.

On the morning of 8 February 1960 she announced she was not feeling well, but a few minutes later was tucking into a large meal. No one, therefore, was worried except Olili, who was on the point of leaving for London on a shopping spree with Barbara Allwright, and as they had arranged to stay the night in London, Olili asked D.P. if she was sure she would not like her to return that evening. D.P. dismissed the idea. 'Don't fuss' was one of her stock phrases.

At 4.30 a.m. the following day Miss Williams popped in to see if all was well, and found her poring over the Racing Calendar. She did not look up from her work and her last words were, 'We must get these entries off to Weatherby's first thing.' An hour later her maid, May, found her dead

A lone figure at the graveside, Olili stumbled as the coffin was lowered, and hands were stretched to prevent her falling into the grave. But with a great effort she recovered her composure and walked away unaided. The woman to whom she had devoted her life was dead and there was nothing left to live for: her brother who had all along disapproved of her life in England, had made repeated efforts to induce her to return to the family estate in Germany, but she had always refused, and they had not corresponded for a long time – there was no one else. For the past year it had been evident that her own health was failing, for she had grown painfully thin but protested there was nothing to worry about. Now that she was alone her will to live had gone, and she surrendered to the disease she had fought so hard to conceal.

Miss Clarke drove the 3.4 Jaguar, appropriately at over 100 mph, to Miss Paget's funeral at Hertingfordbury, and she and her passengers, who were D.P.'s closest friends, knew that she would have approved. Bishop Anthony of the Russian Orthodox Church in London was one of the clergy assisting at the service, and among the many wreaths was one from the White Russian residents in Paris, bearing the simple message 'To Dorothy with our love and gratitude'. Everyone felt her presence very strongly in the church, and when her coffin was being carried to the churchyard it seemed to them that she was saying the words she had repeated so often in her lifetime, 'Don't bump me you fools.'

Index